SO-AEQ-072

WOMEN in SCIENCE

Rachel Carson

Author/Ecologist

Women in Science

Rachel Carson
Author/Ecologist

Dian Fossey
Primatologist

Jane Goodall
Primatologist/Naturalist

Maria Goeppert Mayer
Physicist

Barbara McClintock
Geneticist

Maria Mitchell
Astronomer

WOMEN in SCIENCE

Rachel Carson

Author/Ecologist

E. A. Tremblay

CHELSEA HOUSE
PUBLISHERS
A Haights Cross Communications Company
Philadelphia

CHELSEA HOUSE PUBLISHERS
VP, New Product Development Sally Cheney
Director of Production Kim Shinners
Creative Manager Takeshi Takahashi
Manufacturing Manager Diann Grasse

Staff for RACHEL CARSON
Editor Patrick M. N. Stone
Production Editor Jaimie Winkler
Photo Editor Sarah Bloom
Series & Cover Designer Terry Mallon
Layout 21st Century Publishing and Communications, Inc.

A Haights Cross Communications  Company

http://www.chelseahouse.com

First Printing

1 3 5 7 9 8 6 4 2

Library of Congress Cataloging-in-Publication Data

Tremblay, E.A.
    Rachel Carson / E.A. Tremblay.
        p. cm.—(Women in science)
Summary: A biography of the biologist who helped initiate the
environmental movement.
    ISBN 0-7910-7244-4 HC   0-7910-7520-6 PB
    1. Carson, Rachel, 1907–1964—Juvenile literature. 2. Biologists—
United States—Biography—Juvenile literature. 3. Environmentalists—
United States—Biography—Juvenile literature. [1. Carson, Rachel,
1907-1964. 2. Biologists. 3. Environmentalists. 4. Scientists. 5. Women—
Biography.] I. Title. II. Series: Women in science (Chelsea House Publishers)
QH31.C33 T74 2002
570'.92—dc21
                                                        2002015593

Table of Contents

Introduction

Jill Sideman, Ph.D.
President, Association for Women in Science

I am honored to introduce WOMEN IN SCIENCE, a continuing series of books about great women who pursued their interests in various scientific fields, often in the face of barriers erected by the societies in which they lived, and who have won the highest accolades for their achievements. I myself have been a scientist for well over 40 years and am at present the president of the Association for Women in Science, a national organization formed over 30 years ago to support women in choosing and advancing in scientific careers. I am actively engaged in environmental science as a vice-president of a very large engineering firm that has offices all around the world. I work with many different types of scientists and engineers from all sorts of countries and cultures. I have been able to observe myself the difficulties that many girls and women face in becoming active scientists, and how they overcome those difficulties. The women scientists who are the subject of this series undoubtedly experienced both the great excitement of scientific discovery and the often blatant discrimination and discouragement offered by society in general and during their elementary, high school, and college education in particular. Many of these women grew up in the United States during the twentieth century, receiving their scientific education in American schools and colleges, and practicing their science in American universities. It is interesting to think about their lives and successes in science in the context of the general societal view of women as scientists that prevailed during their lifetimes. What barriers did they face? What factors in their lives most influenced their interest in science, the development of their analytical skills, and their determination to carry on with their scientific careers? Who were their role models and encouraged them to pursue science?

Let's start by looking briefly at the history of women as scientists in the United States. Until the end of the 1800s, not just in the United States but in European cultures as well, girls and women were expected to be interested in and especially inclined toward science. Women wrote popular science books and scientific textbooks and presented science using female characters. They attended scientific meetings and published in scientific journals.

In the early part of the twentieth century, though, the relationship of women to science in the United States began to change. The scientist was seen as cerebral, impersonal, and even competitive, and the ideal woman diverged from this image; she was expected to be docile, domestic, delicate, and unobtrusive, to focus on the home and not engage in science as a profession.

From 1940 into the 1960s, driven by World War II and the Cold War, the need for people with scientific training was high and the official U.S. view called for women to pursue science and engineering. But women's role in science was envisioned not as primary researcher, but as technical assistant, laboratory worker, or schoolteacher, and the public thought of women in the sciences as unattractive, unmarried, and thus unfulfilled. This is the prevailing public image of women in science even today.

Numerous studies have shown that for most of the twentieth century, throughout the United States, girls have been actively discouraged from taking science and mathematics courses throughout their schooling. Imagine the great mathematical physicist and 1963 Nobel laureate Maria Goeppert Mayer being told by her high school teachers that "girls don't need math or physics," or Barbara McClintock, the winner of the 1983 Nobel Prize in Medicine or Physiology who wrote on the fundamental laws of gene and chromosome behavior, hearing comments that "girls are not suited to science"! Yet statements like these were common and are made even today.

I personally have experienced discouragement of this kind, as have many of my female scientist friends.

I grew up in a small rural town in southern Tennessee and was in elementary and high school between 1944 and 1956. I vividly remember the day the principal of the high school came to talk to my eighth-grade class about the experience of high school and the subjects we would be taking. He said, "Now, you girls, you don't need to take algebra or geometry, since all the math you'll need to know will be how to balance a checkbook." I was stunned! When I told my mother, my role model and principal encourager, she was outraged. We decided right then that I would take four years of mathematics in high school, and it became my favorite subject—especially algebra and geometry.

I've mentioned my mother as my role model. She was born in 1911 in the same small Southern town and has lived there her entire life. She was always an unusual personality. A classic tomboy, she roamed the woods throughout the county, conducting her own observational wildlife studies and adopting orphaned birds, squirrels, and possums. In high school she took as many science classes as she could. She attended the University of Tennessee in Knoxville for two years, the only woman studying electrical engineering. Forced by financial problems to drop out, she returned home, married, and reared five children, of whom I'm the oldest. She remained fascinated by science, especially biology. When I was in the fourth grade, she brought an entire pig's heart to our school to demonstrate how the heart is constructed to make blood circulate; one of my classmates fainted, and even the teacher turned pale.

In later years, she adapted an electronic device for sensing the moisture on plant leaves—the Electronic Leaf, invented by my father for use in wholesale commercial nurseries—to a smaller scale and sold it all over the world as part of a home nursery system. One of the proudest days of her life was when I received my Ph.D. in physical and inorganic chemistry, specializing in quantum mechanics—there's the love of mathematics again! She encouraged and pushed me all the way through my education and scientific career. I imagine that she was just like the father of Maria Mitchell, one of the outstanding woman scientists profiled in the first season of this series. Mitchell (1818–1889) learned astronomy from her father, surveying the skies with him from the roof of their Nantucket house. She discovered a comet in 1847, for which discovery she received a medal from the King of Denmark. She went on to become the first director of Vassar College Observatory in 1865 and in this position created the earliest opportunities for women to study astronomy at a level that prepared them for professional careers. She was inspired by her father's love of the stars.

I remember hearing Jane Goodall speak in person when I was in graduate school in the early 1960s. At that time she had just returned to the United States from the research compound she established in Tanzania, where she was studying the social dynamics of chimpanzee populations. Here was a young woman, only a few years older than I, who was dramatically changing the way in which people thought about primate behavior. She was still in graduate school then—she completed her Ph.D. in 1965. Her descriptions of her research findings started me on a lifetime avocation for ethology—the study of human, animal, and even insect populations and their behaviors. She remains a role model for me today.

And I must just mention Rachel Carson, a biologist whose book *Silent Spring* first brought issues of environmental pollution to the attention of the majority of Americans. Her work fueled the passage of the National Environmental Policy Act in 1969; this was the first U.S. law aimed at restoring and protecting the environment. Rachel Carson helped create the entire field of environmental studies that has been the focus of my scientific career since the early 1970s.

Women remain a minority in scientific and technological fields in the United States today, especially in the "hard science" fields of physics and engineering, of whose populations women represent only 12%. This became an increasing concern during the last decade of the 20th century as industries, government, and academia began to realize that the United States was falling behind in developing sufficient scientific and technical talent to meet the demand. In 1999–2000, I served on the National Commission on the Advancement of Women and Minorities in Science, Engineering, and Technology (CAWMSET); this commission was established through a 1998 congressional bill sponsored by Constance Morella, a congresswoman from Maryland. CAWMSET's purpose was to analyze the reasons why women and minorities continue to be underrepresented in science, engineering, and technology and to recommend ways to increase their participation in these fields. One of the CAWMSET findings was that girls and young women seem to lose interest in science at two particular points in their pre-college education: in middle school and in the last years of high school—points that may be especially relevant to readers of this series.

An important CAWMSET recommendation was the establishment of a national body to undertake and oversee the implementation of all CAWMSET recommendations, including those that are aimed at encouraging girls and young women to enter and stay in scientific disciplines. That national body has been established with money from eight federal agencies and both industry and academic institutions; it is named BEST (Building Engineering and Science Talent). BEST sponsored a Blue-Ribbon Panel of experts in education and science to focus on the science and technology experiences of young women and minorities in elementary, middle, and high school; the panel developed specific planned actions to help girls and young women become and remain interested in science and technology. This plan of action was presented to Congress in September of 2002. All of us women scientists fervently hope that BEST's plans will be implemented successfully.

I want to impress on all the readers of this series, too, that it is never too late to engage in science. One of my professional friends, an industrial hygienist who specializes in safety and health issues in the scientific and engineering workplace, recently told me about her grandmother. This remarkable woman, who had always wanted to study biology, finally received her bachelor's degree in that discipline several years ago—at the age of 94.

The scientists profiled in WOMEN IN SCIENCE are fascinating women who throughout their careers made real differences in scientific knowledge and the world we all live in. I hope that readers will find them as interesting and inspiring as I do.

A Voice
in the Silence

As man proceeds toward his announced goal of the conquest
of nature, he has written a depressing record of destruction—
directed not only against the earth he inhabits, but against the
life that shares it with him. . . . Under the philosophy that now
seems to guide our destinies, nothing must get in the way of
the man with the spray gun.
—Rachel Carson, *Silent Spring* (1962)

Rachel Louise Carson had just gotten the news, and she was appalled: *Reader's Digest,* the most popular magazine in the world in 1958, was about to publish an article defending the United States government's policy of spraying clouds of toxic chemicals into the air to kill insects. She was no fonder than anyone else of stinging fire ants or pesky, disease-carrying mosquitoes, but poisons were poisons—and what killed an ant could just as easily kill a bird, a woodchuck, or a human being.

July 8, 1945: The first public test of an insecticide machine, spraying beachgoers with DDT. At the time, the insecticide was considered a marvel of modern science; until Carson's work, especially *Silent Spring* (1962), few if any thought of what the dangers of industrial chemistry might be. Carson's activism sounded a much-needed alarm.

As far as Carson was concerned, DeWitt Wallace, the editor of *Reader's Digest*, should have known better. Back in 1945, before achieving national fame as an author of books about the sea, she had proposed writing an article for the *Digest* about tests that were being performed in Maryland on the powerful pesticide dichlorodiphenyltrichloroethane, or DDT. The tests had hinted at some destructive effects of the chemical, and Carson had wanted to explore these; but Wallace had rejected the idea with no explanation. (Carson had approached him with a similar idea about arsenic in 1938, and he had rejected that as well.)

His attitude toward the research was not unusual for the

time; little was known then about the effects of chemicals on the environment, and the idea of studying these effects had not taken hold. Too, industrial chemistry and other relatively new sciences occupied a place of privilege in the popular imagination: science was widely seen as the way of the future, and the disillusionment with technology that followed such disastrous advances as the atomic bomb had not yet really developed.

DDT had been used first to protect American soldiers during World War II—to combat the malaria-carrying mosquitoes that infested the islands in the South Pacific where those soldiers were stationed. Malaria, caused by a microscopic parasite that lodged itself in the human bloodstream, has killed millions of people throughout history, and it had become a serious threat in the war. At the same time in Europe, DDT was being sprayed directly on those infested with lice. It was the most powerful and effective weapon available against dangerous insects, for whereas most other pesticides could kill only one or two species DDT was effective against hundreds. (The Swiss chemist Paul Hermann Müller, who first adapted DDT as a pesticide, had won a Nobel Prize for his efforts.)

Nothing, however, comes without a price. By 1958, the scientific evidence for the ecological destructiveness of this and similar chemicals was growing, and a recent, unannounced spraying of a mixture of fuel oil and DDT had caused an environmental disaster—a mass killing of small wildlife throughout Pennsylvania, New York, and all of New England. A group of conservationists and landowners from Long Island, New York were preparing to launch a lawsuit to stop the spraying.

It was a case of the U.S. government trying in the wrong way to do the right thing. Government airplanes had sprayed and fogged broad tracts of land all over the northeastern United States the summer before to control mosquitoes, moths, and caterpillars. Now they wanted to stage a second attack against Dutch elm disease, a highly contagious tree fungus that can kill an elm tree in as little as three weeks by choking off the vessels that circulate its water supply. The fungus sticks to the legs of elm-bark beetles, which carry the disease during mating season from tree to tree, and it can move like a plague through an elm forest and destroy it in a single season. In theory, pesticides should stop the spread of the disease by killing the insects that carry it.

By trying to save the forests with DDT, however, the government was causing more problems that it was solving. Not only was the noxious stuff killing beetles, it was also wiping out insects that were beneficial to gardeners and farmers—such as honey bees and grasshoppers—and decimating the local bird populations. To make matters worse, evidence was growing that both the destructive beetles and the local mosquitoes were developing a resistance to the poisons: it seemed that even as it lost its effectiveness against the unwanted insects, DDT was making them stronger.

Carson wasn't surprised by any of this. She'd been thinking about the devastating effects of science on the environment since the obliteration of Hiroshima by the atomic bomb in 1945. The effects of radioactive fallout—tiny dust particles that emit invisible, dangerous waves of radiation—on everything in the natural environment, including people, had been horrendous. She wondered whether toxic chemicals released into the air or water might have the same effects. At first, the ideas that had occurred to her had been difficult to accept; they were, if not too far-fetched, certainly too horrible to entertain. But the years since then had forced her to face reality. In a letter to her close friend Dorothy Freeman, she wrote:

> Some of the thoughts that came were so unattractive to me that I rejected them completely, for the old ideas die hard, especially when they are emotionally as well as intellectually dear to me. It was pleasant to believe, for example, that much of Nature was forever beyond the tampering reach of man—he might level the forests and dam the streams, but the clouds and the rain and the wind were God's. . . .

It was comforting to suppose that the stream of life would flow on through time in whatever course that God had appointed for it—without interference by one of the drops of the stream—man. And to suppose that, however the physical environment might mold Life, that Life could never assume the power to change drastically—or even destroy—the physical world.

These beliefs have almost been part of me for as long as I have thought about such things. To have them even vaguely threatened was so shocking that, as I have said, I shut my mind—refused to acknowledge what I couldn't help seeing. But that does no good, and I have now opened my eyes and my mind. I may not like what I see, but it does no good to ignore it, and it's worse than useless to go on repeating the old "eternal verities" that are no more eternal than the hills of the poets. (*Always, Rachel,* 248–249)

These thoughts had turned into action by 1957, when she learned about a huge expansion in the use of dangerous pesticides by the United States Department of Agriculture (USDA)—a government agency intended to assist and to protect American farms and farmers—in a program to eradicate fire ants. At the request of the president of the Audubon Society, a conservationist group, Carson had helped get the USDA to release its findings on the destructive effects of DDT and other, similar chemicals on natural ecology.

Despite the efforts of Carson and many others who were aware of the problem, the USDA continued inexorably along its track, even announcing plans to expand its program. It was also spraying in the northeastern United States to battle other unwanted insects, such as mosquitoes and gypsy moths.

The people who lived in the paths of these spraying projects grew angry at what seemed like governmental arrogance. One in particular, Beatrice Hunter, wrote a devastating letter to *The Boston Herald* about her experience with pesticide abuse

DeWitt Wallace, here pictured with his wife, was the founder and editor of *Reader's Digest*, one of the world's most popular magazines. Wallace not only declined Carson's offer to write about the dangers of pesticides but also published an article that *supported* the government's spraying policies. The relationship between Wallace and Carson was complex, though, and eventually some of her work would be published in the *Digest*.

and the damage it had caused to wildlife in New Hampshire. Whatever its effect may have been on the mosquitoes, the pesticide had left the land covered with the corpses of songbirds. Olga Huckins, an environmentalist and lecturer and an old friend of Carson's, then wrote her own irate letter to the same newspaper. She and her husband maintained a bird sanctuary around their home in Massachusetts, and as a result of spraying for mosquitoes that had taken place during the previous summer, the birds had been decimated and their breeding grounds contaminated.

With all of this going on, it was impossible to believe that *Reader's Digest* was taking a stand in favor of pesticide spraying. The only explanation was that DeWitt Wallace wasn't convinced by the stories and complaints of all these people in the Northeast. Perhaps he needed stronger, more conclusive scientific evidence. Surely, Wallace was no fool; he and his wife had created and established the most popular magazine in the world. He was known, in fact, to be a remarkably intelligent person, and many called him wise. If he needed proof that the aerial spraying of DDT was dangerous, then Carson considered it her calling to find it for him.

CARSON TAKES ACTION

Carson began her quest with one of the mightiest weapons used by writers and journalists: the telephone. She called the USDA for statistics and research on the poisons used against fire ants. She called the offices of congressmen who were investigating the environmental hazards of insecticides. She called officials of the Department of Health, Education, and Welfare and of the Food and Drug Administration (FDA) to get information about pesticide contamination in the food and water supplies. She called and asked for reports on the chemicals from the National Audubon Society and the Conservation Foundation.

Then she gathered up all her information and wrote a letter to Wallace:

> I cannot refrain from calling to your attention the enormous danger—both to wildlife and, more frighteningly, to public health—in these rapidly growing projects for insect control by poisons, especially as widely and randomly distributed by airplanes. . . . [A] publication with the *Digest*'s enormous power to influence public thinking all over the country would not wish to put its seal of approval on something so potentially hazardous to public welfare. (Lear, 316–317)

With her letter she sent all of the information she had gleaned from her research. If this evidence didn't convince Wallace, she thought, then nothing would.

Her passion over the issue didn't stop with her sending a letter, though; nor was it limited to DDT. Fearing the worst from the cumulative effects industrial chemistry, she extended her crusade to include the rest of the "over 200 basic chemicals have been created for use in killing insects, weeds, rodents, and other organisms described in the modern vernacular as 'pests'":

> These sprays, dusts, and aerosols are now applied almost universally to farms, gardens, forests, and homes—nonselective chemicals that have the power to kill every insect, the "good" and the "bad," to still the song of birds and the leaping of fish in the streams, to coat the leaves with a deadly film, and to linger on in soil—all this though the intended target may be only a few weeds or insects. Can anyone believe it is possible to lay down such a barrage of poisons on the surface of the earth without making it unfit for all life? They should not be called "insecticides," but "biocides." (*Silent Spring*)

The first item on Carson's agenda was to write an article about the Long Island lawsuit. Like any good reporter, she wanted to get her information at the source, so she contacted one of the plaintiffs, Marjorie Spock, whose two-acre garden had been spoiled by planes that had dusted it with DDT 14 times in one day. Spock was a brilliant, articulate person, a born rebel, and a strong believer in organic gardening—gardening without the use of artificial chemicals. She was the daughter of a renowned attorney and the younger sister of the enormously influential developmental psychologist Benjamin Spock. And she was eager to come to blows with those responsible for the pollution.

At the end of each of the 22 days of the trial, Spock dutifully wrote down all she could remember about what had gone on that morning and afternoon in the courtroom. Then, making reproductions on an early, experimental model of a fax machine, she sent copies to all her friends and other interested parties, including Carson.

One of Carson's key traits was her determination. Gifted with eloquence, she used her skill at communication to make the public aware of dangers to which, disastrously, no one was paying attention.

Until that time too few scientists had taken the problem seriously enough to do research on it, and by the trial's end the plaintiffs' evidence on the effects of pesticides on the environment had not satisfied the presiding judge. To make matters worse, the government had brought in its own scientists and experts, as well as agricultural officials, who claimed that aerial spraying did no harm to the environment whatsoever and treated the plaintiffs as uneducated eccentrics. After three weeks, the judge dismissed the case.

Carson was disappointed but not defeated. The courts weren't the only battlefield on which this war could be waged; there was also the public forum. Carson was sure that educating the populace about insecticides would increase public outrage and thus support for her cause. She approached E.B. White, a famous staff writer for the magazine *The New Yorker*, and asked him to pen an article about the problem. White lived in Maine and had certainly seen the damage aerial spraying could do. He responded sympathetically to Carson's request, but he said he wouldn't be able to do the article on his own. He suggested that Carson approach the editor of *The New Yorker*; if she could convince him that such an article would be appropriate for the magazine, then the editor would assign someone skilled to write it.

Carson had no such intention; the topic was too important. For her, the time had come to stop following and start leading, so she resolved to write the article herself. In fact, she decided to make the article the centerpiece of an entire book about the dangers of chemical pollution.

The decision to write the book was momentous: the book would change both Carson herself and the field of environmentalism forever.

2

A Child's World Is Full of Wonder: 1907–1925

A child's world is fresh and new and beautiful, full of wonder and excitement. It is our misfortune that for most of us that clear-eyed vision, that true instinct for what is beautiful and awe-inspiring, is dimmed and even lost before we reach adulthood. If I had influence with the good fairy who is supposed to preside over the christening of all children I should ask that her gift to each child in the world be a sense of wonder so indestructible that it would last throughout life. . . .
—Rachel Carson, *The Sense of Wonder* (1965)

The clapboard farmhouse in which Rachel Carson was raised in Springdale, Pennsylvania may have been tiny, but the 65 acres of rolling, unspoiled land around it seemed to stretch to the edge of the world. Just up the hill stood an orchard of apple and pear trees, affectionately called "Carson's Grove" by the towns-folk. With equal affection, the Carson family welcomed people

Carson was raised in Springdale, Pennsylvania, near the Allegheny River. There was ample opportunity on the more than 65 acres surrounding her family's farmhouse to observe nature and its creatures. Her curiosity led her to a fascination with living animals, although she discovered a fossil of a seashell near her home that touched off an interest in marine life as well.

from miles around to congregate there for picnics on warm Sunday afternoons, especially in late summer when the fruit trees were in full blossom. Beyond the orchard were abundant woods, meadows, gullies, and streams. Down the hill, to the south of the farm, just beyond the village and behind a stand of pines, flowed the mighty Allegheny River.

The natural world of the local countryside was a wonderland to a child of Carson's inclinations. For as long as she could remember, she had been under its spell, captivated by the mysteries of anything wild that crawled, ran, flew, or swam. She knew under which rocks she would find salamanders sleeping, and which logs were home to rattlesnakes and copperheads and therefore best avoided. She explored the banks of ponds populated by frogs, turtles, carp, and otter; and streams full of minnows, darters, crawfish, and beavers. In the woods in autumn, she would sometimes catch sight of a white-tailed deer, a bobcat, or even the occasional red fox, and the paths among the trees were always alive with chipmunks, rabbits, squirrels, opossums, and porcupines. She knew there were black bears, too, although luckily she'd never run into one of those.

She and her mother, a clever, strong-willed Scots-Irish woman who had always professed her own fascination for the natural world, often went birdwatching together. Carson had held in her palm the delicate pale blue shards of a hatched robin's egg from an abandoned nest—knowing that only a month before, a mother robin would have been defending that same nest against marauding blue jays and kestrels, swooping in aerial battles among the oaks, pines, maples, and birches. She saw bluebirds, flycatchers, thrushes, tanagers, swallows, woodpeckers, hummingbirds, warblers, and orioles. Sometimes she would spot grouse, killdeer, falcons, owls, geese, and, on lucky days, wild turkeys. And there was almost no thrill like the brilliant red-black-gold-brown of a rooster pheasant suddenly surging upward from the tall grass of a field and into the air.

The creature that would ultimately capture her imagination most, however, was not a live animal, but the petrified remains of a dead one. Ancient fossils of sea animals were abundant in the Allegheny River basin, and many of the local children collected them for fun. One day, when she was barely more than a toddler, Carson went for a walk with her mother; along the way discovered the fossil of a large seashell in an outcropping of rock. The discovery set Carson's mind ablaze with questions, not the least perplexing of which was that of how a sea animal had become stuck in a rock high up on a hill. Had there once been an ocean here? If so, then what had happened to it?

It was perhaps at that moment that the greatest fascination of her life was born inside of her: a fascination with the world beneath the waves. Many years later, when her passion for studying marine life had brought her fame and fortune, Carson would remark that she couldn't remember a time when she hadn't felt this interest, that it had been with her since she was a little girl.

But although her life out of doors was full of wonder, her life in the house was not. The entire family—Rachel and her mother, father, older sister, and older brother—all had to squeeze into two bedrooms, each of which was barely large enough to lie down in. (The situation would deteriorate when Carson was eight years old: Marian, her sister, was married then and installed the new husband in the house with everyone else.) The ground floor comprised a small parlor and dining room, separated by a central staircase. There was no indoor plumbing. For fresh water and refrigeration, the family used a springhouse, located about 50 feet from the main quarters. Two outhouses served hygienic needs. The kitchen was a lean-to, with a gas stove and a table but no running water. A small cellar with an outside entrance served to store fruits and vegetables. A fireplace at either end of the house provided some heat in winter, but the bedrooms were kept warm with small coal-burning stoves.

Around the house, plant life flourished. The eastern corner at the rear of the building was practically invisible underneath a grape arbor. Wisteria and honeysuckle climbed two sides of the raised front porch as if it were a trellis. Just off the porch grew a lilac bush, a mulberry tree, and a vegetable garden. The family had also planted pear, maple, and birch trees nearby.

Carson's parents had never intended to make their home a working farm—her father had hoped the place would turn out to be a profitable real estate investment—but they did keep some animals, including a few chickens, sheep, and pigs and a horse. A coop, a barn, and a stable housed the animals, and the

The Carson family, photographed perhaps while Robert Carson, an insurance salesman, was away on one of his many travels. Marian is at the far left, followed by Rachel and Maria and the younger Robert. Rachel's brother would enlist in the Army Air Service in 1917, and the 10-year-old Rachel would adapt one of his war stories for the *St. Nicholas* League.

young Carson fell as deeply in love with these creatures as she did those of the forest.

She would never have recognized at her young age that life on her family's farm was anything but ideal, but in fact, life was a struggle for her parents. Carson's father, Robert, who was an insurance salesman by profession, would have genteelly claimed that although he was not rich, he was at least keeping up with expenses; but the state of the farm made it clear that the Carsons were poor. Not all the bills were paid. Robert Carson was rarely able to stay at home because his business kept him on the road most of the time, while his wife had to earn what little extra money she could by giving piano lessons on an instrument that had somehow been squeezed into the parlor.

Music was one of the few things in Maria Carson's life that gave her comfort in those days, and Rachel shared her mother's passion for it. The two of them would spend hours together, singing songs to Maria's accompaniment, while the two older children were in school.

THE EARLY WRITINGS

Rachel also loved to draw and write, and one of her first creations was a pasted-together book that combined all of her interests: nature, storytelling, and art. She used flour and water to bind the book's ten pages together, and she entitled her effort *The Little Book for Mr. R.W. Carson*. She wrote an introduction for it: "This little book I've made for you my dear, I hope you'll like the pictures well; the animals that you'll find here—About them all—I'll tell." (Lear) With a little help from her mother, she used crayons and pencils to fill the book with pictures of animals she loved—whether she had encountered one or not—including a mouse and an elephant.

The book was a portent of things to come. When Carson was eight, she wrote a short story entitled "The Little Brown House," which centered on a birdhouse. The following year, she wrote another, which she called "A Sleeping Rabbit." She illustrated a cover for both tales with drawings that were obviously influenced by illustrations in her favorite magazine, *St. Nicholas*; at the time, this was by far the leading children's magazine in the nation.

St. Nicholas had been founded in 1872, on Dr. Josiah

Gilbert Holland's idea of creating a magazine for children that would be full of stories, poetry, and articles. Other children's periodicals of the day had similar formats, but Holland would hold this one to a much higher literary standard. He presented his proposition to the publishing house Scribner's, and the editors there decided to make his idea a reality. They appointed Mary Mapes Dodge as editor-in-chief.

Dodge had been a successful writer of children's stories herself, her most famous work being *Hans Brinker, or the Silver Skates* (1865). When she was given the job of developing the new magazine, she chose *St. Nicholas* as the title, after the patron saint of children, and she made it clear from the beginning that she did not want to see in the magazine's pages the pontification, the sermonizing, that was so common in children's literature at the time. She wanted the magazine to be a forum in which for children to amuse themselves as they wanted to, a collection of literary odds and ends that would both inform and entertain. She also insisted on having the work illustrated by the best popular artists of the time.

The magazine sponsored a kind of organization to which children contributed their own stories, essays, songs, and poems; this was called the *St. Nicholas* League. Many of the children who published stories there, including F. Scott Fitzgerald, Rudyard Kipling, Mark Twain, and E.B. White, went on to become some of America's most famous writers as adults.

Carson first published a story of her own in *St. Nicholas* in 1918, when she was 11 years old. She called her tale "A Battle in the Clouds," taking her inspiration from a story her brother, who had just joined the Army Air Service, had told her about a Canadian pilot who had been shot down over France by a German plane. Thousands of American boys had gone to Europe to fight in the Great War—World War I—so such stories were immensely popular at the time.

After she submitted her story, she had to wait nearly five months to find out whether it had been chosen for publication.

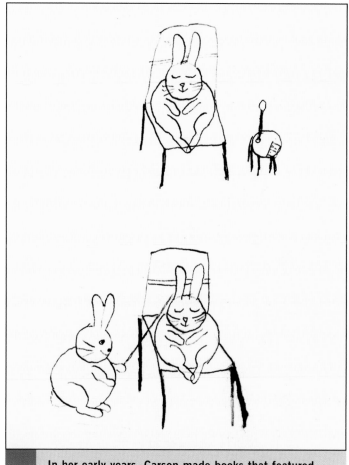

In her early years, Carson made books that featured pictures of animals. She became a published author at the age of 11, when a war story she'd written appeared in the children's publication *St. Nicholas*. She won several awards for her writing, which inspired her to pursue writing more regularly, and she started earning money consistently for her writing at the age of 14.

The news finally came—the September issue contained the full text of "A Battle in the Clouds." And not only was she now a published author, she was also a prize-winning one, for she had been awarded a silver badge for excellence in prose.

One success led to another. In the following year, Carson published two more stories in *St. Nicholas,* both about the war. The first was entitled "A Young Hero." The second, "A Message to the Front," won her the coveted gold badge of excellence.

The last piece she published in that year was an essay, "A Famous Sea Fight," which described the American victory over Spain at Manila Bay during the Spanish-American War. After publishing so many pieces within a single year, the *St. Nicholas* League made her an "honor member" and awarded her a small cash prize.

THE CODE OF *ST. NICHOLAS*

In running *St. Nicholas,* Mary Mapes Dodge had a very specific idea of the kind of magazine she wanted to maintain—what she wanted it to offer and how she wanted her readers to react to it. She summarized her editorial policy as follows:

- To give clean, genuine fun to children of all ages.

- To give them examples of the finest types of boyhood and girlhood.

- To inspire them with an appreciation of fine pictorial art.

- To cultivate the imagination in profitable directions.

- To foster a love of country, home, nature, truth, beauty, and sincerity.

- To prepare boys and girls for life as it is.

- To stimulate their ambitions—but along normally progressive lines.

- To keep pace with a fast-moving world in all its activities.

- To give reading matter which every parent may pass to his children unhesitatingly.

Dodge never changed this policy.

Once she had actually received money for her writing, her future course was set. She had always wanted to be a writer, and now she knew she had the talent to realize her dream. Two years later, she received her first paycheck for writing—money paid not as a prize, but as regular compensation for her work. She had submitted an essay to *St. Nicholas* in the usual way, but this time the editor replied that although it wasn't appropriate for the League, he would like to put it to good purpose in publicizing the magazine. He offered her a penny a word. Needless to say, she accepted his offer, becoming technically a professional author at the tender age of 14.

PARNASSUS AND PITTSBURGH

At the same age, another momentous event occurred in her life: she enrolled in high school. Unfortunately, Springdale was too small a town to support its own secondary school, so most children either commuted by train to schools in other communities or went off to boarding school. Carson was too poor for either option; boarding schools were expensive, and so were train tickets. Instead, she went to private tutoring sessions offered to ninth- and tenth-graders at the local elementary school.

She didn't seem to mind. Undaunted by her circumstances, she continued to meet the high academic standards she had always set for herself. Throughout elementary school, she had been a straight-A student, and nothing changed when she made the transition to the ninth grade.

Her parents, who couldn't help recognizing how special their youngest daughter was—both of the older children had dropped out of school after the tenth grade—made the financial sacrifice of sending her by trolley to Parnassus High School, several miles away. Only 44 students attended the school, and nearly two thirds of them were girls. Once again, she achieved excellent grades, but she never managed to establish much of a social life. She was extremely shy—a characteristic she'd developed after her family's increasing poverty had become

Carson initially took private tutoring sessions for ninth-graders. Eventually, her family sacrificed financially for her to attend Parnassus High School, but she was shy and didn't socialize much there. She maintained high grades, as she had done in her previous years in elementary school; outside of academics, she enjoyed playing field hockey and basketball.

the subject of local gossip. But being often alone was second nature to her. She had always spent more time caring for her farm animals and exploring natural habitats in the wild than she had socializing with other people. She did, however, enjoy sports—she played field hockey and basketball—and as the other kids came to know her a little better and saw beyond the quiet, solitary exterior she usually presented, they came to like and appreciate her.

When it came time to graduate in June of 1924, she felt some small regret at leaving Parnassus, but it was time to move on to bigger and better things. She had been accepted to the Pennsylvania College for Women (PCW) in Pittsburgh.

Pittsburgh was a steel town, a tough, brawny place, where smoke and ash from the local mills choked the residents and filled the air with a constant haze. On some days, the cloud of pollution that hung over the town grew so thick that the buildings could not be seen even from the city limits.

The campus of PCW wasn't any better. Although it was located a good 10 miles up the road from the steel mills, prevailing winds carried the soot and acrid smell through the windows of every dormitory and classroom. It found its way into the students' hair and clothing and irritated their eyes and skin. It presented a special problem for Carson, who had come to campus already suffering from an extreme outbreak of acne. Her hair was so thick that it would have been the envy of her classmates had it not become a trap for the sooty filth that filled the air. All in all, her appearance didn't make a terribly good impression on her classmates, but she had been a loner for so long now that she didn't even think about what kind of impression she made. To Carson, the important things in life were intellect and achievement. And as long as she was true to those values, she felt, life would provide whatever she needed.

In fact, life had recently done just that. Her family could never have paid all of her college tuition. A few years before, her father had given up selling insurance for a commission and took a low-paying job as a switchman with the West Penn Power Company. Her mother had taken on more piano students. And a plan had been afoot to sell off property from the farm to raise cash. But the combined incomes of both of Carson's parents

The steel town of Pittsburgh, Pennsylvania, shown here in 1926. Her time at PCW was Carson's first exposure to pollution on a grand scale; in fact, her book *Silent Spring* (1962) would be a major factor in later clean-air legislation.

still added up to a meager sum, and the property sale wasn't as successful as they had hoped. Instead, Carson had won a scholarship of $100 per year from the State Department of Instruction to help with her tuition, and because of her obvious capabilities and her achievements in high school, friends of the president of PCW quietly donated funds that paid off a large part of the balance of her expenses.

The president of the college, Cora Coolidge, was always doing favors like this for her girls. She was fiercely committed to them and to the ideal of giving young women a higher education. She was a New England Yankee who had graduated with honors from Smith College and gone on to study at other centers of higher learning all over the world. She wanted to give other women the same opportunities she'd had.

Coolidge made a formidable presence around the campus. She was heavy-set, with a thin, no-nonsense mouth and wide, clear eyes. She wore wire-rimmed spectacles and a chignon of silvery hair at the back of her head. Her usual bearing was imperious and even intimidating; but when she broke into a smile, which she often did, she seemed more like a doting grandmother.

And many of the young women thought of her in that way. They knew that she was their champion and mentor and that she would do anything for her girls with a completely open heart—provided they didn't smoke or let their grades slip. When she contacted personal friends to help with Carson's financial situation, she did it secretly, so it came as an utter surprise to Carson that most of her tuition had been paid.

With money problems no longer a distraction, Carson felt free to throw herself completely into her studies. Unlike her classmates, many of whom expected to graduate college and then go on to become homemakers and mothers, Carson was determined to use her education to help her fulfill her life's dream: to become a full-time professional writer. She thought she knew the path her life would take. She would write great stories of the sea, in the tradition of her favorite authors, Herman Melville, Joseph Conrad, and Robert Louis Stevenson. She would be famous and rich and happy. Her dreams felt like destiny.

Carson sailed through her freshman year, "aceing" all her subjects, playing basketball and field hockey, and going to tea with her brilliant English Composition teacher, Grace Croft. She also published a sea story, "The Master of the Ship's Light," in the college literary magazine. She expected that her sophomore year would progress in much the same way.

Then the unexpected happened. The guidelines of the academic program at PCW required that all undergraduates take a core of basic courses, including two semesters of science. Carson may have thought of herself as a budding novelist, but when she stepped into a science classroom her life turned completely around.

3

Where Poetry
Meets the Sea:
1925–1935

Awareness of ecological relationships is—or should be—the basis
of modern conservation programs, for it is useless to attempt
to preserve a living species unless the kind of land or water it
requires is also preserved. So delicately interwoven are the
relationships that when we disturb one thread of the community
fabric we alter it all—perhaps almost imperceptibly, perhaps so
drastically that destruction follows.
—Rachel Carson, "Essay on the Biological Sciences" (1958)

MARY SCOTT SKINKER

Few things are as attractive as passion, and Mary Scott Skinker,
Carson's sophomore science teacher at PCW, had a passion for
biology. Carson had never met anyone like her. Skinker was tall,
elegant, stylish, and even a little mysterious. As she stood at the
front of the classroom, lecturing in her soft, ardent voice on the
characteristics of species and phylum, the eyes of her students

As a woman interested in pursuing her career, Mary Skinker, a biology teacher at PCW, became not only Carson's mentor but also a close friend. Carson caught her passion for biology, and Skinker's class can be said to have changed radically the course of Carson's life.

would always fix in fascination on the flower pinned among the tresses of her gathered chestnut hair. She wore a new one every week. Everyone guessed they came from a secret admirer, but try as they might, the girls couldn't penetrate the identity of the gentleman. They could only guess at what a worldly, charming Galahad he must be to have caught the eye of someone like Miss Skinker, for she would never have given a second glance to anyone less worthy.

Nor did the girls have any idea as to why a woman as beautiful and accomplished as she was would choose a life of teaching, thereby sacrificing the satisfactions of a husband and family. Of all the rare and exotic creatures about which she lectured, she was perhaps one of the rarest of all in those days— a career woman. She had been born in Denver, Colorado, but her family soon moved to St. Louis, Missouri, where she spent her childhood. After her graduation from her own high school, she taught for 12 years in the local high schools. Eventually, she moved east to New York and earned a master's degree in science from Columbia Teacher's College, then a master's degree in zoology from Columbia University. When she landed a job at PCW, she quickly became a presence to be reckoned with on campus, a "mover and shaker" who would champion her students in any battle but also held them to the highest of academic standards.

If Miss Skinker was a puzzle to many of her students, Carson had put at least some of the pieces together. Both women had been drawn off the set courses of their lives by a fascination with science. Carson could see in her teacher the same passion for the creatures of nature that she herself had felt since childhood. And as Miss Skinker had turned away from an ordinary life to pursue her passion, Carson found herself, for the same reason, turning away from her dream of becoming a storywriter.

GIVING UP WRITING ALTOGETHER?

In her secret moments, Carson would have to admit that her love of science wasn't the only reason she was giving up on a life of writing literature. She was beginning to believe that she didn't have the talent to become a truly great writer. The more she wrote, the more she felt that her writing lacked imagination. And giving up the idea of becoming a famous author didn't prove as difficult as she might have thought. After all, literature and science were fundamentally the same to her, in that they both represented paths on the quest for truth. As she would say many years later, accepting the 1952 National Book Award for *The Sea Around Us*:

> The materials of science are the materials of life itself. Science is part of the reality of living; it is the what, the how, and the why of everything in our experience. It is impossible to understand man without understanding his environment and the forces that have molded him physically and mentally.
>
> The aim of science is to discover and illuminate truth. And that, I take it, is the aim of literature, whether biography or history or fiction.

In any case, it wasn't as if she were giving up writing for good. Quite the opposite: she wrote a story for *The Englicode* that earned her a campus literary prize at the end of the year.

As usual, Carson did well academically during her second year at PCW, and when she returned in the fall, she was lucky enough to have classes with both her mentors, Miss Skinker in biology and Miss Croft in composition. Unfortunately, she also took an elective course in secondary education, in which she earned the lowest grade of her academic career— a B–. Obviously, she wasn't cut out to be a high school teacher, but she wasn't much bothered by that. She had never given that particular career choice any serious consideration.

What she did have to consider seriously, though, was whether to change her major from English to science. In the 1920s, few people believed that women were intellectually capable of keeping up with men in the scientific fields, so a career as a scientist was for them almost pure fantasy. Still, Carson couldn't deny her enthusiasm for biology, and writing had become more and more like a chore. She'd much rather spend those hours looking through the lens of a microscope in a laboratory than cuddling up with a novel in the library.

Amidst all the rebirth and renewal of spring, as the

dogwoods and cherry trees blossomed, the birds once again began to sing, and rabbits played tag on the lawns of the campus, Carson decided it was her time for self-renewal as well: she dropped a literature course, replaced it with one in chemistry, and changed her major to zoology.

She was worried about what her mother would say. After all, she had received her scholarship based on taking an English major with a focus in writing. Both her family and President Coolidge expected her to become an author, not to go chasing rainbows in science, a field in which she might not even be able to make a living. But there was one person, at least, who would be absolutely filled with joy at the news: Mary Skinker. That was enough for Carson.

Skinker was indeed overjoyed at the good news, but she had some disappointing news to offer in return. She had decided not to return to PCW the following year. Rather, she would take a year off and pursue her doctoral degree at Johns Hopkins University in Baltimore. She needed the degree in order to continue to pursue her career as a college professor, and lately she and President Coolidge hadn't been getting along very well. A year's absence would provide a good cooling-off period for both of them.

Carson was devastated, of course, but she remained undaunted. She looked up to Mary Skinker more than any other person in the world. She immediately decided she would skip her last year of undergraduate school, forego her bachelor's degree, and follow Skinker to Johns Hopkins to work directly on her master's degree. Skinker didn't object. In fact, the two young women seemed to become closer than ever as they confided their hopes and dreams for the future to each other. Skinker even revealed the identity of her secret admirer—an officer in the German Air Force who was brother to a professor of German language at PCW. She also revealed that she intended to break off the relationship. This summer, before she started graduate studies, she would be doing research at the Marine Biology Laboratory in Woods Hole, Massachusetts, so there would be no time to spend with a suitor.

All would have been well but for one stumbling block: finances. Carson would need a scholarship to attend Johns Hopkins, and a substantial one. The school, as it turned out, was willing to give her financial support, but not quite enough for her to get by. She was heartbroken. She would have to maintain her contact with Skinker only through letters.

At least she still had Miss Croft, her composition teacher, to help and guide her. Or so she thought. When she returned to school at the beginning of her senior year, she learned that Grace Croft had resigned her position at the college, for reasons unknown.

Now, except for a few friends who shared her interest in science, she felt completely alone. Miss Skinker's replacement was not adept at laboratory work, which had to be Carson's concentration that year. So Carson did what she had to do: if she couldn't get much help from her teacher, she would make progress on her own. For the next nine months, she remained glued to her microscope, with almost no help or guidance from anyone. When at last she graduated, in 1928, she did so with honors.

Now she would follow in her mentor's footsteps, almost exactly. She had reapplied to Johns Hopkins, and this time, with Skinker's help, she was able to get a full scholarship, as well as an appointment to a seat at the Marine Biological Laboratory in Woods Hole, Massachusetts for the summer.

The Marine Biological Laboratory (MBL) had been founded in the previous century and served as the field laboratory of the U.S. Department of Fisheries. It was one of the few scientific institutions in the United States to admit women on a basis equal to that of men, and it attracted famous and accomplished biologists from all over the world. It contained a huge library and gave researchers access to

The Marine Biological Laboratory in Woods Hole, Massachusetts. Before she began graduate study at Johns Hopkins University, Carson spent a summer conducting research here; hers was one more in a long line of illustrious minds trained at Woods Hole.

countless varieties of marine animals. But perhaps best of all, in Carson's eyes, was that the MBL was situated so close to the ocean; for all her love of maritime stories, she had never before been to the sea.

Carson's position at the lab was as a "beginning investigator," and as such, she could continue some independent research on the nervous system of turtles that she had started when she was in her last year of college. In her off hours, she spent wonderful times exploring the nearby beach and tide pools with her friend Mary Frye, another student from PCW who had won a seat at the MBL. But more importantly, she got to spend time with a well-known researcher in marine biology from Johns Hopkins, Reinhart P. Cowles. It was he who helped her figure out how to go about doing her research. In her last year at PCW, with no one to teach her advanced laboratory techniques, she had not been able to learn some of the skills she now felt she needed, but Cowles took her under his wing.

It was a great summer for her. She voraciously learned new things every day not only about marine life but about lab technique as well. By the end of her stay, she had met famous scientists from all over the world, but the ones she felt were most important to her own future were from the U.S. Bureau of Fisheries, which seemed, from all she had heard, a fantastic place to do research. All in all, her time at the MBL proved to be one of the most productive and enjoyable times in her life.

When she returned home, Carson had only a few weeks to spend with her family before heading for Baltimore and Johns Hopkins. She wasn't sure how she would cope with being separated from her mother for an entire school year. Being apart for the past few weeks had been difficult enough. She was also worried about her father's health. She wasn't sure just what was bothering her, but something about the way he looked was raising her concern. Maybe it was just that he had become more silent and withdrawn lately. He had never been talkative, but now he seemed to turn completely inward.

To make matters worse, Mary Skinker wouldn't be at the university, either. She had suffered health problems in the previous year and had been forced to withdraw from full-time study at Johns Hopkins. When Cora Coolidge at PCW learned of Skinker's situation, she did not react with kindness; after all, Skinker had taken a year's leave of absence to earn a graduate degree, not to sit around her home all day, drinking tea. Eventually, the situation led to Skinker's severing her ties with PCW. There were other places that would appreciate her talents and abilities. In the meantime, she pursued her graduate studies on a part-time basis at George Washington University. She would need that graduate degree if she ever expected to land another job in academia.

When Carson arrived at Johns Hopkins, she learned to her delight that her faculty advisor would be none other than Reinhart P. Cowles, the scientist who had been her mentor at Woods Hole. With his blessing, she set right to work, continuing her laboratory explorations of reptilian nervous systems—which she hoped would prove a fruitful subject for the graduate thesis she would have to write to earn her degree.

WOMEN AT WOODS HOLE

Carson was one of many women who studied or did research at the Marine Biological Laboratory (MBL) at Woods Hole. At a time when science was dominated by men, the MBL took the courageous stand of opening its enrollment to qualified applicants of *both* sexes. From the institution's founding in 1888 until 1910, women accounted for approximately one third of the total enrollment. The number of female applicants decreased after that and remained low until the 1970s. Woods Hole has never granted degrees to its students, but many of the women who have studied there have gone on to earn doctoral degrees at other institutions of higher learning.

Of all the women who spent time at the MBL, Carson was not the only one to become a famous writer: Gertrude Stein, one of the great innovators of 20th-century literature, also studied at Woods Hole, just after her graduation from Radcliffe College. At the time, she had been considering a career in medicine. To this day, Woods Hole continues to attract talented women scientists from all over the world.

JOHNS HOPKINS, THE DEPRESSION, AND THE PEARL LAB

Graduate school immediately proved a far greater challenge than PCW had ever been, especially with courses like organic chemistry—widely considered by students there to be their most difficult hurdle. Carson had to struggle just to earn a B in the course, but it was a B she was very proud of.

Her other struggle was more personal. She missed her mother and family, who were still up in Springdale, suffering like everyone else the financial ravages of the Great Depression—a huge downturn in the nation's economy that happened in the late 1920s and lasted until the United States entered World War II in 1942. Carson wanted to do something to get them out of that place and down to Baltimore with her.

As far as she was concerned, she would just as soon never return to Springdale. What had once been a beautiful country-side of farms and woodlands along the banks of a great river had over the years slowly transformed into an ugly community of power plants, factories, and cheap housing developments. The Eden of her childhood had disappeared forever.

If she intended to move her entire family to Maryland, however, she would need more space than the room she now occupied. She would have to find space not only for her father and mother but also for her brother, her sister, and her sister's two children from a previous marriage. Carson went on a house hunt. It didn't take her long to find one, in Stemmer's Run, located within walking distance of the Chesapeake Bay. It had lots of room, a big fireplace, a tennis court, and indoor plumbing. By summer, the entire family—with the exception of her brother, Robert, who had remained behind to handle the sale of the Springdale property—had moved in.

The summertime proved no less busy for Carson than had the regular school year. She landed a teaching assistantship at the university, working with Grace Lippy, a brilliant young biologist who had also been a protégé of Cowles and was now going on to obtain her doctorate. Grace was brash, lively, and assertive; her demeanor complemented the gentle diplomacy with which Carson would handle the problems of the summer-school students so well that inevitably, the two young women became close friends. That proved a relief to Carson, as she had no other friends at the place.

The summer went by quickly, and Carson now had her mother's help in handling domestic chores, so she had more time to devote to her work. The fall, however, brought a new problem: tuition was increasing, and her scholarship wouldn't cover all of the increase. She would have to find a job.

One of the first places she looked was the Institute for Biological Research, which operated under the auspices of the Johns Hopkins medical school. The Institute had been founded by a famous student of the university named Raymond Pearl, who was somewhat of a genius in the study of the biology of groups. The research there was entirely geared toward studying the relationship between general biology and the biology of human beings. Pearl passionately believed that the biology of humans, especially those forces that affected the human life span, was completely intertwined with the ecology of all of nature. Pearl's laboratory was extremely well-funded, and it impressed Carson as a first-class professional facility. When she learned that Pearl happened to be hiring lab assistants, she jumped at the chance to work for him.

Although her new job proved interesting, it also stole much of her time away from academics and lab work, making it that much harder to succeed in those areas. As always, her way of dealing with the pressure was to try even harder, but she knew that eventually something would have to give. For now, that "something" was time spent in the lab working on her research of reptilian nervous systems. The research had not been going well to begin with—she wasn't getting the kind of results and information from it that she would need to complete her master's thesis—so it was almost an obvious choice for the

Johns Hopkins University. Mary Skinker went from PCW to Johns Hopkins to pursue her doctoral degree. Carson was initially disappointed that her professor was leaving PCW, but she followed her mentor to Baltimore. With Skinker's help, Carson won a full scholarship. She worked as a beginning investigator at the Marine Biological Laboratory, the field laboratory of the U.S. Department of Fisheries, under Reinhart P. Cowles. After completing her thesis, she received her master's degree in 1932.

"back burner." But putting off her research presented a problem: the longer she waited, the longer it would take to graduate. The longer it took to reach graduation, the longer she would have to wait to look for full-time employment. In the meantime, her financial situation was growing worse and worse. She just wasn't earning enough to meet all her expenses, and the other members of her family were bringing in no income whatsoever. Not that they weren't trying—her brother was doing whatever automotive work he could find—but employment was hard to come by during the Great Depression.

When her job at Pearl's laboratory was eventually eliminated, she was lucky enough to find—with the help of Professor Cowles—another job, at the Dental and Pharmacy School at the University of Maryland. In the meantime, Professor Cowles helped her in another way by suggesting a new topic for her master's thesis, one that would be easier and quicker to complete, and more likely to yield useful results than had her study of reptiles. This time she would be investigating the urinary systems of fish—actually trying to discern the functions of a kidney-like organ in certain species. To her relief, the experiments went well and led to an essay that was praised by academic referees—professors who judge original academic work. At the end of 1932, at long last, she received her master's degree.

She had hoped this would lead to employment possibilities. It didn't. She ended up spending the summer with Grace Lippy, first teaching another graduate course, then going with her to Woods Hole for another six weeks of research. When she came back, she decided to apply to the Johns Hopkins doctoral program.

She also returned to teaching at the University of Maryland, but the income wasn't enough to sustain her academic career and her family. After two more years of hard work and dedication, she realized she had taken on too much. Her brother had moved out, so she had one fewer mouth to feed, but her sister had become severely diabetic and disabled. Her father's health also seemed to be declining. She had to use her time to find another way to bring in extra income, so she withdrew from the program at Johns Hopkins.

This was a low point for Carson. Her dreams of becoming a research scientist seem to be evaporating before her eyes. But something good did come out of the situation: she reawakened her old interest in writing. To earn extra money, she took out stories she'd written several years before and sent them off to magazines known to pay high rates for fiction. The stories were rejected, but upon rereading them, Carson discovered she was a much better writer than she had realized—and her interest in writing was rekindled.

Hope seemed to blossom anew for Carson, if only in that small way, when fate stepped in and dealt her the most tragic blow she had ever felt: one morning her father shuffled into the kitchen complaining that he was feeling a little out of sorts. This wasn't unusual. His health had been declining steadily over the past couple of years. But when he stepped outside, hoping to catch a breath of fresh air, he seemed to stumble, and then fell to the ground. Carson and her mother rushed out to help him, but it was too late. Robert Warden Carson, age 71, had died.

4

The Dance of Science and Art: 1935–1941

The winds, the sea, and the moving tides are what they are. If there is wonder and beauty and majesty in them, science will discover these qualities. If they are not there, science cannot create them. If there is poetry in my book about the sea, it is not because I deliberately put it there, but because no one could write truthfully about the sea and leave out the poetry.
—Rachel Carson, accepting the
National Book Award for Nonfiction, 1952

THE BURIAL

Carson's father had never really provided for his family in life. Now, in turn, they couldn't provide for *him* in death. He had failed as an insurance salesman and as a land speculator, so when he passed away, he had nothing to leave—not even insurance money for his own funeral. Carson talked the matter over with her mother and two siblings, but in the end, there was nothing

The Carson family was always very poor. Robert Carson, an insurance salesman, was usually on the road, and while he traveled his wife taught piano lessons to supplement their meager income. Later, Robert became a switchman for the West Penn Power Company—but the entire family still had to squeeze into two cramped bedrooms. Rachel began to worry about her father's health when he became more withdrawn than usual; at the age of 71, he stumbled out of the house and collapsed. His burial was left to relatives who could afford to pay for it.

much to discuss. They simply couldn't afford to bury him.

On the other hand, Maria wouldn't allow the man she had married and loved for all of her life to be buried in "Potter's Field," that section of public cemeteries where poor people were interred, often without so much as a grave marker to remember them by. After all, he had not been a *bad* man, just an unsuccessful one. She had rushed to his side when he collapsed in the yard, kneeling by him and resting his head in her lap, stroking his hair and secretly praying that he would open his eyes and everything would be all right. But everything was not all right, and now they would have to send him home to Pennsylvania. He had siblings of his own there. It would be up to them to take care of the funeral arrangements.

Neither his wife nor his children would escort the body, for every penny spent on travel was one fewer to spend on food or housing. So they would have no opportunity to say goodbye to their father as he was lowered into the earth or hear any kind words spoken in his memory. He would simply be loaded onto a train, and they would stand at the station watching him disappear unceremoniously from their lives forever.

In some ways, although no one would say so, the death of Carson's father came as a blessing. With so little family income, having one fewer mouth to feed eased the burden on Carson, if only by a little. But the relief was temporary—only slowing, not stopping, the family's slide toward financial disaster. Something needed to be done. Carson couldn't depend on her brother; he was living on his own now, working only occasionally, and uninterested in helping to support his mother, sisters, and nieces. Her sister, Marian, was far too sick to work at all, so she couldn't contribute, either. And her mother, of course, was simply too old. The responsibility was Carson's alone.

THE BUREAU

Finding a better job in order to raise the necessary funds would be no easy task. She thought about teaching at the college level, but a master's degree wouldn't take her very far in the academic world. The same would be true of research institutions and natural history museums, where the jobs for women were scarce in any case. One possibility did hold some promise, however: she might be able to work for the government.

Mary Scott Skinker had done exactly that. After she had finished her doctoral work at George Washington University, at 40 years of age, she'd felt too old to start a new career in academia. She had turned, then, to the U.S. government—the largest employer of scientists and researchers she knew. She had passed the civil service examinations in her field, which were specialized tests given to anyone who wanted to work in the employ of the United States, and had accepted a full-time job with the Department of Agriculture's Bureau of Animal Industry.

Carson was impressed with how happy Skinker seemed at the Bureau, and in turn Skinker strongly encouraged Carson to take some of the civil-service exams offered to zoologists. It didn't take much convincing. Carson took four exams in various fields, and she scored well on all of them. Unfortunately, her performance meant only that she would be considered for a full-time position when one came along. No one knew when that might be.

Carson seemed at an impasse, but Skinker came to the rescue once again. Knowing how deeply Carson loved all things about the ocean, Skinker suggested that she pay a visit to Elmer Higgins, who ran the Bureau of Fisheries for the U.S. Department of Commerce. In fact, Carson had been introduced to Higgins once before, on one of her many visits to Washington to visit Skinker, and he had been extremely impressed with her.

When Carson sat down with Higgins to discuss employment opportunities, she thought at first that she had stumbled into another dead end. He had no full-time jobs available. He did, however, have a project with which he needed help. In fact, it had been giving him headaches ever since he'd taken it on. His superiors had assigned him the task of creating a year's worth of short, weekly radio programs—52 seven-minute segments in all—that would help to educate the public about marine animals and what the Bureau of Fisheries was contributing to their management in coastal waters.

Elmer Higgins, head of the Bureau of Fisheries. Carson met him through Mary Skinker's suggestion, and he hired her to create 52 radio segments a year to educate the public about marine animals and coastal water management—a perfect blending of her interests in writing and the ocean. When she'd proven her abilities with the radio segments, Higgins asked her to write educational brochures for the Bureau; the result was too literary, so he suggested that she send it to *The Atlantic Monthly* and start over on the brochure.

The problem was that no one at the Bureau knew anything about writing for the public. When scientists tried their hand at the project, which had been named *Romance Under the Waters,* they created boring, overly complex, and technical scripts. When professional writers had their turn at it, they couldn't quite grasp and communicate the scientific content the scripts needed to communicate. Now Higgins had taken on the monumental task of writing all the programs himself, but he had so much else to do at the Bureau that he couldn't dedicate to the project the time it really deserved.

If Carson could perform as she promised she would on this project, she would be a godsend to Higgins. Here was a person who not only knew marine biology but who could also put words together in an interesting, entertaining way. She seemed perfectly suited to the job.

And she jumped at the opportunity. The pay was unremarkable—an extra $13.00 for two days of work each week—but it was better than nothing, and she was now the first in line for any full-time job that might open up within the Bureau. She enjoyed the project, too, as it combined her two favorite things in all the world: writing and learning about the ocean.

For his part, Higgins knew he was taking a risk by giving the assignment to Carson. After all, he didn't know her well, and he couldn't be sure that she would be able to achieve the necessary marriage of science and literature. But he had a hunch about her. She was reserved, but she was obviously self-assured where her qualifications were concerned. And Mary Scott Skinker had spoken very highly of her.

As soon as he read her first two scripts, he put his worries to rest. Carson obviously knew how to write, and the necessary scientific information was all there. As far as he was concerned, she had the job for as long as she wanted it.

Work on *Romance Under the Waters* went on for another eight months, which greatly helped to relieve the financial difficulties of the Carsons, since Rachel still had an income from teaching part-time at the University of Maryland. But even greater relief came in other ways. Once Carson started writing again, the floodgates of her creativity seemed to open. She began writing articles about sea creatures for *The Baltimore*

Sun, a newspaper in the area, and for her first one, she received a payment of $20.00.

Higgins was so impressed with her writing that he asked her to contribute material for an educational brochure for publication by the Bureau of Fisheries—and the final draft she submitted was far too well-written, too poetic, for a simple government brochure. Higgins gently suggested that Carson have another try at the brochure, and that she submit the manuscript of her first attempt to *The Atlantic Monthly,* a famous literary magazine. The effect of this validation on Carson was enormous; the affirmation was so gratifying that she set to work on Higgins' proposal without delay, rewriting the brochure as he wanted it along the way.

She had once told herself that she had given up writing completely, but now she was slowly beginning to realize that she had simply put her literary pen away until she had found a subject she thought worth writing about. She didn't submit her article to the *Atlantic.* Instead, she put it away so that she could take it out when she felt more objective about it and could make corrections. Eventually, she sent it off to *Reader's Digest,* but they never gave her the courtesy of a reply. It didn't matter. She could write. She knew that now.

CARSON AS JUNIOR BIOLOGIST

In July of that year, 1936, after working on radio scripts for eight months, Carson got the opportunity she had been waiting for. A new entry-level position had been funded for the Bureau. She couldn't be absolutely certain she would land the job, of course, even though she had scored well in the civil service exam. Only one other woman was employed there at the professional level. She felt a little as if she were applying to an all-male club. Higgins spoke on her behalf, however, so she was offered the job of junior biologist.

Her duties required that she log and analyze statistics on coastal fish populations and that she continue to produce the

Carson's position as a junior biologist at the Bureau of Animal Industry brought some financial stability to her life at last, and at this point she began to understand that she could merge her science and her writing in a meaningful way. After her sister's death and a move to Maryland came Carson's breakthrough as a writer: the sale of "The World of Waters" to *The Atlantic Monthly*.

same high-quality educational brochures she had been creating as a part-time employee, only now she came into work every day and received a weekly paycheck. She also continued to contribute articles on marine science to *The Baltimore Sun*.

Professionally, Carson began to feel comfortable. Financially, her mind was now far more at ease. But her home life was headed for another tragedy. Carson's sister had grown more and more ill since moving to Maryland. Not only was Marian diabetic, but she had also become chronically depressed. She had gone through several bad marriages, was mothering two daughters who were now about to enter adolescence, and had no skills with which to support herself. Unlike Carson, she had always depended on men for support, and unfortunately, the men she had chosen had not been at all dependable.

Now she seemed to have given up on everything. Day after day the spark of life within her seemed to dwindle, until now it was hardly more than a flicker. When pneumonia struck that winter, she had no defenses to mount against its attack. She grew sicker and weaker until finally, a few weeks after New Year's Day in 1937, Marian died.

Carson mourned the loss of her sister. The girls had been more than 10 years apart in age, and Marian had never shown any interest in living the life of the intellect, but Carson had felt a close bond with her nevertheless. Also, Marian's two daughters, Virginia and Marjorie, would now become Carson's responsibility. Her mother would help to raise them, of course, but Maria was in her 70s now, and there was only so much she could do. The weight this placed on Carson's shoulders was heavy indeed, but she never shirked it for an instant. She had come to love the girls—after all, she had lived with them throughout their lives—and she would be the best parent to them she knew how to be.

Gradually, the gloom in the house lifted, and life returned to normal. Maria watched over the girls during the day, so that Carson could go to work. Work, however, was stealing more and more time from home life because Carson now had to make frequent trips to Washington, D.C. to spend time at Bureau headquarters. Traveling the long distance by bus could take hours out of her day. So, as much as she adored living near her beloved Chesapeake Bay, she quickly came to realize that it was time to move.

She found a small place in Silver Spring, Maryland. Silver Spring was a bedroom community for Washington and Baltimore, so it was much more densely populated than Stemmer's Run had been. Carson preferred the quiet and the natural beauty of the Chesapeake Bay area, but her new home wasn't unpleasant, and it gave her easy access to work in both cities and in College Park.

A new start in a new home must have inspired her to renew her writing efforts as well, because she soon took out the essay she had written for the department a year before, which she called "The World of Waters," and decided to take Higgins's advice: she would try to sell it to *The Atlantic Monthly*. She read it over, did some revising, and then sent it off.

THE FIRST BIG SALE

On July 8, 1937, Carson made the first important breakthrough of her literary career. She received word from the editor of *The Atlantic Monthly*, Edward Weeks, that the magazine wanted to buy the article. She was ecstatic, of course, but the letter of acceptance

A MAGAZINE OF FIRSTS: THE ATLANTIC MONTHLY

Carson had reason to be especially proud of her publication in *The Atlantic Monthly*, for it had a long history of discovering great new writers. Henry James and Mark Twain both published first in its pages, and Edward Weeks, the editor who bought Carson's "Undersea," also bought and published Ernest Hemingway's first short story, as well as the first English translations of stories by Vladimir Nabokov. Even the founders of the magazine were among the most honored forces in American literature; they include Ralph Waldo Emerson, Henry Wadsworth Longfellow, and Oliver Wendell Holmes, who gave the magazine its name. Among its other firsts, the *Atlantic* paid Julia Ward Howe a $5.00 fee when it became the first periodical to publish "The Battle Hymn of the Republic," which later became the anthem of the Confederacy during the American Civil War.

awakened the perfectionist in her. When Weeks suggested making a few minor changes to the text, Carson, driven to turn her science writing into true art, revised and rewrote right up until the day of her deadline. The piece was published under the title "Undersea," a change suggested by Weeks.

One thing led to another. Among the readership of *The Atlantic Monthly* was Quincy Howe, a senior editor at Simon & Schuster, a famous book publishing company in Manhattan. He was so impressed with Carson's writing that he wrote to ask if she planned to write a book on the subject of marine life. She received another letter of praise from Hendrick Villem van Loon, a highly respected author who was already established at Simon & Schuster.

With so much interest in her writing, she knew she had to move quickly to take advantage of the opportunities coming her way. She immediately went to work on a proposal for a book about the ocean, and she accepted an invitation to visit van Loon and his wife in Connecticut. From the tone of his letters, Carson knew he had been discussing her writing with Howe.

When she finally made it to van Loon's home in January for dinner, Howe and his wife showed up as well. From the moment she arrived, she knew they had decided to publish her book, and it was all she could do to hide her excitement. They talked about various ways she might go about approaching her topic. The next day, Carson and Howe met at the offices of Simon & Schuster to continue the conversation.

Howe soon agreed to offer her a contract on the basis of her outline and several chapters from the book, but he didn't offer any advance money, so her victory was bittersweet. As always, she needed funds to support her family, so she would have to concentrate on writing feature articles for the Baltimore papers as well as an occasional article or book review for *The Atlantic Monthly.*

For months to come, her feature writing would take up all of her free time. The book would have to wait. She wrote about

Carson spent a 1938 vacation near the U.S. Fisheries Station in Beaufort, North Carolina, near the Outer Banks, where she became devoted to her explorations of the coastline. The sight of the life in the water affected her so profoundly that she vowed to communicate her wonderment to her readers. The result was *Under the Sea-Wind*, a book that remains influential today.

fish, and shore birds, and conservation. She wrote about pollution and wildlife management and ecology. And of course, as she was doing all of this writing, she continued her full-time work with the Bureau. It was a grueling schedule. When she finally decided to take a vacation in July of 1938, her mind was ready for a complete change of scenery and habits.

She spent her vacation with her mother and two nieces near the U.S. Fisheries Station in Beaufort, North Carolina, near the Outer Banks. It was here, with no writing to do for the papers and no research to complete for the Bureau, that she had a sudden awakening, an enlightenment that seemed to arise out of her exhausted state of mind. What happened was simple: she discovered a glorious ebb and flow of life among the sand dunes and tidal pools. She spent hour after hour exploring

Carson experienced a kind of epiphany on the beach near Beaufort—
she became fascinated with the life in the tidal pools, spending day and
night exploring and learning about these creatures. She called on these
observations in writing *Under the Sea-Wind*.

every hidden nook of the beach in her search for creatures, struggling for survival in this primal, natural habitat. What she found moved her deeply. As she later admitted to a close friend that while watching "young mullet pouring through that tide race to the sea" she stood "knee-deep in that racing water and at times could scarcely see those darting, silver bits of life for my tears." (*Always, Rachel*, 281)

Unsatisfied with simply spending all of her daylight hours among the dunes, she began to explore at night with a flashlight, finding scenes of the nocturnal life of birds, crabs, fish, and insects she never would have dreamed of otherwise. Mentally, she took volumes of notes. All of this would all show up in her book.

A year later, in June of 1939, she finally received a promotion to assistant aquatic biologist at the Bureau, although owing to governmental politics—all of the bureaucracies were undergoing massive reorganization—she ended up working back at College Park for only $200 more a year. The reorganization eventually brought together the Bureau of Fisheries with another bureau, the Biological Survey, to make them into one unit, the U.S. Fish and Wildlife Service.

Despite all the changes and frustrations she had to endure during the reorganization, being shuffled from one location and supervisor to another and meeting opposition everywhere simply because she was a woman, she fared much better than her old friend Mary Skinker. Skinker had been doing research work on parasites for the Division of Zoology in the Department of Commerce, but she had ultimately locked horns with a new boss who held the old-fashioned belief that a woman's place was in the home. Apparently, his constant teasing and harassing became unbearable for her, so that she finally resigned her job and moved to New York, where she took a position at Columbia Teacher's College.

Skinker was lucky. She had landed a job interpreting surveys and statistics, and rewriting reports and brochures based on information the Service was gathering about fish on the East Coast. Little by little, she was becoming an expert on the oceans she wanted to write about in her book.

It was during the summer of 1939 that Carson finally had enough of her book done to send along a first chapter and outline. Howe, on behalf of Simon & Schuster, offered her a $250 advance. She could have used more, but she was a first-time author, and the publisher wasn't about to risk a large sum on a newcomer. She accepted the offer. It was time to get to work on her book, which she decided to call *Under the Sea-Wind*. A new adventure in her life was beginning.

5

This Little Book I've Made for You: 1941–1952

It is a wholesome and necessary thing, for us to turn again to the earth and in the contemplation of her beauties to know the sense of wonder and humility.
—Rachel Carson, *The Sense of Wonder* (1965)

UNDER THE SEA-WIND

Under the Sea-Wind **was published in November of 1941.** Carson had high hopes for the book, of course. However, as van Loon reminded her, any new book was a gamble and there was no predicting what the reading public might take to and what it might not.

The literary critics loved the book, which told of the life and death of sea birds, a mackerel, and an eel and was written in a style that readers recognized as both poetic and scientifically accurate. Scientists also praised *Under the Sea-Wind,* and even today it remains an indispensable guide to for people who

Carson's first major literary breakthrough came when she edited the essay she had written for Higgins, which she called "The World of Waters," and sent it to *The Atlantic Monthly*. The magazine bought the article and published it under the title "Undersea." A few years later, in 1939, Carson had enough of her book done to submit the first chapter and outline of *Under the Sea-Wind* to Simon & Schuster, for which she received a $250 advance.

skin-dive or otherwise explore reefs, coves, and inlets.

Critically, the *Under the Sea-Wind* was a huge success. Financially, it was not. The book didn't sell many copies. It had been on the store shelves for only a month when the Japanese attacked Pearl Harbor and the nation's attention turned to its own survival. Ecology and zoology were peacetime interests. The conservation of fish and birds had little to do with armies and navies. Once President Roosevelt announced a declaration of war, all thoughts were on the safety of fathers, sons, and husbands who would be shipping off to foreign lands, where they would fight and perhaps die.

In addition to hurting the sales of her book, the war exerted another profound effect on Carson's life. With the government mobilizing for defense, more and more office space was taken over by the U.S. War Department. Bureaucracies that were not directly connected to the war effort were forced to find office space elsewhere. For Fisheries, that meant moving to Chicago.

Carson wasn't happy about the move, but it turned out to be somewhat easier than she expected because her nieces, Virginia and Marjorie, didn't accompany her. They were young women now, just out of high school and beginning work careers, and there was no reason for them to move to Chicago. They were able to make arrangements to stay in Silver Spring with friends. Carson's mother, Maria, would come along, of course, and Carson would be glad to have her.

Just before the move west, another piece of good luck came in the form of a promotion to assistant aquatic biologist. The extra income would significantly help reduce some of the financial pressure Carson bore.

When they reached Chicago, Carson and her mother found a small, brick house to rent in a suburb called Evanston. It was a comfortable place, but it was a thousand miles from the nearest ocean, and the proximity of Lake Michigan didn't make up for that. Carson was not happy. At least she would still be working with Higgins, but most of her responsibilities centered around writing publicity releases rather than the scientific work she so enjoyed. She was bored. If she didn't find something else to do, she would go crazy.

She did her work conscientiously, of course, but she always kept looking for another job opening that might take her back east. The wait was not long. Eight months after moving to Chicago, she applied for an opening as an associate aquatic biologist in the Office of the Coordinator of Fisheries in Washington, D.C. Because Higgins did the hiring, she was accepted immediately. Soon thereafter, she and Maria were back living in Maryland, in a tiny house in Tacoma Park, not far from her old Silver Spring home.

She received another sizable salary increase, but her work responsibilities didn't change much—she was still writing informational pamphlets. Six months later, she was promoted again, this time to aquatic biologist. But even though she had come back home and her career seemed to be going well, she felt restless. The workload took up most of her energy, and the only time she was able to do more creative writing was late at night. Consequently, she lived on the verge of exhaustion much of the time, leaving her more vulnerable to annoying colds and other passing illnesses.

FINDING THE DREAM AGAIN

If she could have changed careers at that point, she would have done so in an instant. Her old dream of becoming a full-time writer had resurfaced, although she had given up on authoring books. She had learned her lesson from *Under the Sea-Wind.* No matter how good the writing and no matter who praised it, the ultimate success of a book depended on factors that would be completely out of her control. It was better to write short pieces for magazines, for in that situation it was not necessary to sell a certain number of copies in order to earn royalties. Magazines paid in a lump sum, and several of them paid quite well.

Her first big sale, an essay called "The Bat Knew It First," described the similarity of a bat's radar—which allowed it to fly and hunt in the dark—to modern radar. She received a hefty check for her work, and then another from *Reader's Digest,* which bought the rights from her to reprint the article. After that, the Office of War Information bought the rights to distribute the article to its news media offices overseas. Carson's job with the government put her in a unique position to write this kind of article, because the research she reviewed daily at work gave her ample material to draw on.

After the bat essay, she wrote a story about a bird called a "chimney swift," which she soon sold to *Collier's,* a popular magazine of the day. But whatever the advantages, the government wasn't where Carson wanted to be, and she had by now grown confident enough in her writing to believe she could land a job elsewhere.

She applied first to DeWitt Wallace at *Reader's Digest,* but

DEWITT WALLACE AND *READER'S DIGEST*

Carson's relationship with DeWitt Wallace was love–hate through most of her professional career. Although he did enthusiastically publish some of her writing in his magazine, *Reader's Digest,* at other times he failed even to respond to her queries. Still, she never refused to publish there, even once she'd built a reputation.

The idea for *Reader's Digest* came to Wallace while he recovered from wounds he'd received in World War I. An explosion of information had suddenly become available to the general public—far too much for the average reader to keep up with. Wallace felt that by condensing the essentials of this information into a single monthly periodical, he could help the average reader to keep abreast of many issues at once. He circulated his idea unsuccessfully, and finally he and his wife, Lila, published the magazine on their own. *Reader's Digest* has since become the most widely read magazine in history, with over 100 million readers and editions in 19 languages. Wallace died in 1981.

although he liked her work, he had no openings at the time for an editor. Toward the end of 1945, she applied for a job with the official magazine of the National Audubon Society, a privately funded group dedicated to the conservation of birds, but nothing came of it.

Prospects for a new job outside the government were growing dimmer by the day. With the war finally coming to an end, she would be competing with returning war veterans for every opening, and she, as a woman and a non-veteran, would certainly be at a disadvantage.

It was also in 1945 that she had her first brush with information about the destructive effects of DDT on the environment. Reports on the chemical, which had come across her desk, concerned her. Scientists at the Patuxent River Research Refuge were studying the effects of DDT on beneficial insects and other wildlife. So far, the results had been frightening. Not only was it destructive to small animals, birds, and beneficial insects, but it also persisted in the environment for long periods. Carson offered to write an article on the subject for Wallace at *Reader's Digest,* but he wasn't interested. The general public wasn't interested in hearing bad news, after all. They had just gone through a war, and they needed topics that offered a more optimistic message. Carson dropped the idea of writing an article for the time being, but the topic never ceased to concern her.

If Carson's professional life didn't seem to undergo any immediate improvement with her return to Washington, her social life certainly did. For the first time ever, she found herself among a broad circle of friends, people she had come to know both at the Service and at the Audubon Society. She took field trips and nature hikes, went to parties and gatherings, shared meals and innermost secrets. She might once have claimed that she was happy being a loner, but she had to admit, she was thoroughly enjoying herself in the social whirlwind.

After a few months, she also had to admit, her work had become more enjoyable as well. She had been given greater responsibility and a staff of six assistants to manage. Frequently, she had to travel to other locations or go out in the field to do research. Her salary had finally become a livable wage. But still, she was sure she had more to offer. The only way she could do that, as far as she could figure, would be through publishing, but as it turned out, authoring articles just didn't pay enough. Perhaps it was time to consider writing books after all. A book might fail financially, as her first book had, but it might also succeed beyond her wildest imagination. She decided to give the notion some thought, and ideas began to percolate in the back of her mind.

When Carson felt creative, her inspirations overflowed into every facet of her life, including her job. With the enthusiastic blessing of the new head of Fish and Wildlife, Albert M. Day, Carson sketched out a plan for a series of 12 booklets that would describe to the public how the government carried out a conservation program through its wildlife refuges. They would call the series *Conservation in Action*. The project would require quite a bit of travel, mostly to visit refuges that would be included in the pamphlets, but for Carson, traveling to new places appealed to her sense of adventure.

CONCERVATION IN ACTION

Carson's first trip, in 1946, was to the refuge in Chincoteague, Virginia, along the "Eastern Shore" of the Delmarva Peninsula. She brought with her a good friend from Fish and Wildlife, an illustrator named Shirley Ann Briggs, a lively, optimistic young woman who had a deep interest in birds. Together they trudged through the marsh and sand of the area to observe shore birds and by boat visited and took notes on the oyster and clamming industries that prospered nearby. It was an exhilarating experience and whetted Carson's appetite for more travel. She would have plenty of it over the next year.

Carson proposed and received approval to write a series of 12 educational booklets that explained the government's conservation program through its wildlife refuges. The series, *Conservation in Action*, would require travel to several of the refuges; here glossy ibises forage at the Chincoteague refuge in Florida.

Her next trip was not an official one. She had been a government employee for 10 years now, and according to official policy, she was now owed a year's leave to pursue research or whatever else might interest her. Carson, however, didn't want a year off. She wanted a month's vacation, paid for by the department.

She got her wish. She packed up her bags and cats, and with her mother in the passenger seat, drove north to the Sheepscot River in Maine, just outside of Boothbay Harbor. There she rented a cottage, sight unseen, from a local real estate agent. She no sooner laid eyes on the place than it cast its spell on her. It was tiny—a kitchen, a sitting room with a couple of bunk beds, a cramped attic with two more beds, and a screened-in front porch—but she had lived in tiny places before. What made the cottage so marvelous was that from its perch above the banks of the river, it afforded a breathtaking view, and the bird life in the area was as rich and varied as she could have hoped for, with warblers, and thrushes, and starlings of every variety. What was just as important, in her eyes, was that only a short five-mile drive separated her from the rocky coastline. She was always irresistibly drawn to any place where the land met the ocean and tide pools formed. She made that drive every day, and by the end of her stay there, she knew she would return as often as she could. The coast of Maine would hold her in its spell for rest of her life.

Just before the end of her vacation, she entered a contest sponsored by the magazine *Outdoor Life*, which would reward the best effort at creating a conservation pledge that young people could take. She quickly dashed off a few words, spent some time reworking and polishing them, and then sent her finished piece off in the mail:

> I pledge myself to preserve and protect
> America's fertile soils, her mighty forests
> And rivers, her wildlife and minerals,
> For on these her greatness was established
> And her strength depends. (Lear, 137)

Two months later, she received congratulations from the editors of the magazine. The prize, to her delight, was a check for $1000.

She spent most of the rest of that year and the next traveling to other refuges across the country. She made trips to Massachusetts, North Carolina, Utah, Montana, and Idaho. When all the traveling was done, she produced some of the finest nature writing in the pamphlets that anyone in the department had ever seen. The series proved a huge success, both with the public and with her peers.

Carson wasn't quite as successful in another vital area in her life: her health. The stress of so much travel and work left her with a series of minor health crises that culminated in a bad case of shingles—a painful, blistering skin condition caused by the same virus that causes chickenpox. As a result, she had to absent herself from the office for several weeks, during which time she fell further behind in her work.

Even before her absence, her workload had become a challenge. Now it was overwhelming, and it looked as if it would get worse when, in 1949, her boss was promoted and she took over his job as chief editor of the Service's publications. Luckily, she had hired some good people the year before who could help her now—in particular, Bob Hines, a wildlife illustrator who not only proved himself a good employee but also had become a close friend. Part of her workload was self-imposed: Carson had never given up the idea of writing another book, and ever since returning to Washington from her travels she had been sneaking off to the library at night to conduct research.

WRITING ABOUT NATURE

It was still Carson's dream to become a full-time writer, and she confided her dream to an old friend from the Service, Charles Alldredge. Alldredge had been an information officer with the government for many years before retiring to become a freelance speechwriter in 1947. He knew what had happened to Carson's first book, and he often heard from her how her publisher had done almost nothing to promote it. He suggested that she find a literary agent to represent her. Carson had never considered doing such a thing before. In her literary life, she saw herself as a loner. But Alldredge cajoled her until she gave in.

He offered her a list of names, and she reluctantly inter-
viewed several of the people from it. She expected nothing to come
of the interviews, but one of the agents had actually piqued her
interest. The agent's name was Marie Rodell. Carson wasn't quite
sure what attracted her so strongly to this woman. The two were
nothing alike. Carson had been a small-town girl, still rather shy,
with little time for or interest in socializing. Rodell, on the other
hand, was a New Yorker through and through: cosmopolitan,
sophisticated, well-traveled, charming, and an absolute tigress in
representing her clients. She also exuded a natural honesty. Carson
could sense almost at once that here was a person she could trust,
a person she could confide in. She was also obviously bright,
had business savvy, and wouldn't be anybody's pushover in book
negotiations. Even before the interview was over, Carson felt
she had made a new friend.

Tragically, shortly thereafter, she also lost an old one. A few
weeks earlier, word had come from Chicago that Mary Scott
Skinker was dying of cancer. She and Carson had never lost
touch. And Carson had continued to look up to her as an ideal
and mentor. Skinker had ended up going to Evanston to take a
position at the National College of Education, an institution
dedicated to training elementary school teachers for their jobs.
At the beginning of the third month of her first semester there,
Skinker had collapsed to the floor of her campus apartment.
She had been rushed to the hospital, and there, on regaining
consciousness, she'd asked for Carson.

On hearing the news, Carson immediately took a leave of
absence from the Service and boarded a train west. When she
arrived, she went directly to the hospital and took her place at
Skinker's bedside. She never revealed what memories and feel-
ings the two shared during those few brief days together, but
she remained at her old friend's side until Skinker slipped into
unconsciousness.

Now the news came that Skinker had finally drawn her last
breath. The loss was devastating for Carson. She had felt closer

Mary Scott Skinker, Carson's sophomore science teacher at PCW, had a contagious enthusiasm for science and biology. Skinker, in addition to being a mentor to Carson, was a career woman, a rarity in those days. After receiving her doctoral degree, she accepted a job with the Department of Agriculture's Bureau of Animal Industry; both she and Carson had stints with the U.S. government. When Skinker eventually died of cancer, Carson was by her side.

to Skinker than perhaps anyone in the world, with the exception of her mother. But she soldiered on. She had no choice. And instinctively she knew that in Marie Rodell she might have found someone who would fill the void in her life.

REGAINING THE MOMENTUM

Rodell filled the void in more ways than one. At the same time she became Carson's friend, she also became her taskmaster. Together they sat down and formulated a plan that would finally move Carson aggressively into her literary career. The first item on the agenda was to clear up any remaining legal issues Carson might have with Simon & Schuster regarding an option—the right to publish her next book. Then they would find a way to finance a leave of absence for Carson, so that she would have time to finish the project without interruption. Perhaps she could get a grant or fellowship. Finally, they would have to find her a new publisher.

Within a short time, Simon & Schuster had given up rights to any book Carson might write; the Eugene Saxton Memorial Foundation had offered her a grant; and Oxford University Press had expressed interest in publishing *Return to the Sea,* which was the working title of her new book. Clearly, Rodell knew how to get things done.

After that, Carson's life became a whirlwind. She made a trip to Florida with Shirley Briggs to go deep-sea diving, and while there, for the first time, she actually saw the sea floor she had so often pictured in her mind. She also made a day trip through the Everglades on a six-wheeled contraption built by a local explorer. Almost immediately afterward, she took Rodell on a deep-sea expedition out of Woods Hole, Massachusetts. When she finally received the money from the Saxton Foundation, she took time off from work and completed the book, now entitled *The Sea Around Us.*

Parts of it were printed in *The New Yorker, Reader's Digest, Science Digest,* and *The Yale Review.* All of these sales brought in extra money—far more than Carson had ever made in an entire year working for the service. The chapter that had appeared in *The Yale Review,* entitled "The Birth of an Island," won the prestigious George Westinghouse Science Writing Award. Just before publication, it was chosen as a Book-of-the-Month Club selection, which would greatly boost sales. When Oxford Press finally released the book, it became an instant bestseller, remaining on the *New York Times* list for 81 weeks.

By 1952, Carson's name had become a household word in America. Taking advantage of the publicity, Oxford re-released *Under the Sea-Wind*, and this edition too became a bestseller. Among other awards, Carson won the National Book Award and the coveted Burroughs Medal, given for excellence in science writing, for *The Sea Around Us*.

At last she achieved what she had always wanted: the opportunity to put aside her government work and dedicate her life to writing about nature. And it was certain that the time in which she was living desperately needed clear writing about science and the conservation of nature. After all, just a few years before, the world had witnessed the detonation of the first atomic bomb, and, as Carson realized, the country now was capable of obliterating all life from the face of the earth.

6

The Edge of the Sea: 1952–1957

On all these shores there are echoes of past and future: of the flow of time, obliterating yet containing all that has gone before; of the sea's eternal rhythms—the tides, the beat of surf, the pressing rivers of the currents—shaping, changing, dominating; of the stream of life, flowing as inexorably as any ocean current, from past to unknown future.
—Rachel Carson, *The Edge of the Sea* (1955)

Carson had always assumed that becoming a best-selling author would give her the freedom to write that she had always dreamed of. So how could it be, she asked herself, that she now had less time to write than she'd had before?

She was learning quickly that the price of fame was time. Her every hour, every moment seemed to belong to someone else. There were so many invitations to give speeches, accept honors and awards, and attend parties and official functions

When Carson wrote *The Sea Around Us*, parts of it were published in *The New Yorker, Reader's Digest, Science Digest,* and *The Yale Review.* The income generated from these excerpts was more than she had ever made in an entire year. In addition to the financial windfall, the book itself was a bestseller, staying on the *New York Times* list for 81 weeks and making her a household name. With the sales momentum *of The Sea Around Us,* her publishers re-released her previous book, *Under the Sea-Wind.* This time, the book became a bestseller. Carson's writing awards included the National Book Award, the Burroughs Medal (for excellence in science writing) and the prestigious George Westinghouse Science Writing Award.

that she hardly had time to breathe, let alone retreat to the shorelines she loved. Of course, it was difficult to complain about realizing your lifelong dream, and she would never be rude to people who meant only to honor her achievements, but sometimes, she confessed to Rodell, she felt more than a little overwhelmed. After all, if she continued on this way, she would never have a moment to write another word. Is that what her readers really wanted?

Some honors, of course, she was more than happy to accept. She had been given honorary doctoral degrees in science from three colleges, including the Drexel Institute of Technology (now called Drexel University), a famous scientific, technical, and engineering school in Philadelphia; Oberlin College, the first institution of higher learning in the country to accept female students and to promote female teachers to full professorship; and PCW, her alma mater. She also accepted an honorary doctorate in literature from Smith College, a college for women in Massachusetts. She was flattered to receive many other, similar offers, but she politely turned them down, accepting only the four degrees that held personal meaning for her. Drexel represented high achievement in science; Oberlin, the acceptance of women into higher education; Smith, her success as a writer; and PCW, her return home as a conquering hero.

The accolades continued to flood in. Carson was elected to the Royal Society of Literature in England; she received a Distinguished Service Medal from the U.S. Department of the Interior; she was given honorary membership in a national fraternity of women journalists; and she received several more book awards. Finally, however, she realized she had to set limits. After talking over her decision with Rodell, she began declining invitations to speaking engagements. She needed time to write. After all, she had already made commitments to a new publisher, and she was long overdue on fulfilling them.

THE SHORELINE BOOK

Two years before, when she had finished the manuscript for *The Sea Around Us*, she had come up with an idea for another book; she had presented this to Oxford, but Oxford had turned it down as too expensive to publish. Marie Rodell had then sent

Carson to propose her idea to Paul Brooks, then editor-in-chief at the publishing house Houghton Mifflin in Boston.

Carson and Brooks were simpatico from the start. He'd read some of her work and was absolutely entranced by it. Even better, he had recently been looking for someone to write a guide to creatures that lived on and near the shoreline along the East Coast—and the same idea had been percolating in Carson's mind for quite some time. They agreed that she would write the book, and Carson immediately contacted her old friend at Fish and Wildlife, Bob Hines, to illustrate it.

The problem then had been one of time: after the publication of *The Sea Around Us*, there simply weren't enough hours in the day to research and write the book for Houghton Mifflin.

But two years had passed since that episode, and now that she had reclaimed her time, she would finally be able to begin the project in earnest. She also divested herself of some financial burdens, which had been claiming far too much of her attention. If for most of her life she had had too little money, she now had too much. She owed so much in taxes that she was forced her to hire an accountant to look after her affairs. When she learned that a fellowship she had been granted by the Guggenheim Foundation had been declared taxable income by the Internal Revenue Service, she decided to give the money back. She didn't need the trouble of accepting it, and other deserving people could put the money to better use.

Carson traveled north to begin her research for her new book, to the coast of her beloved Maine. She took Bob Hines with her to make some preliminary sketches. Afterward, she headed south to the Carolinas, then on to the Florida Keys. When she had finished this phase of her fieldwork, she had voluminous notes on the creatures that lived in four very different environments: rocky coast, sandy beach, marshland, and coral reef. Each species had its own ecology and relationship to the surrounding environment, which is what most interested Carson.

These corn seeds, contaminated by mercury, illustrate just the effect Carson dreaded: when consumed by birds, they can disrupt the food chain severely.

When she returned home from Florida, she realized that she had made so much progress and enjoyed herself so much that it was time to make a momentous decision about her future. It was time, she felt, to leave her job at Fish and Wildlife. She conferred with her mother and with Marie Rodell, and they both agreed. So on May 7, 1952, Carson sent off her letter of resignation. It was a moment she had dreamed about for years. Now she was completely on her own.

As there was no longer any reason for her to remain close to Washington, D.C., she moved with her mother to a rented house in Woods Hole, Massachusetts. The marine research laboratories were conveniently right across the street, and she could travel with ease to Maine to do further research on the coastline there.

It was on one of these jaunts to the North that she found herself looking for a house to buy. After all, she could afford a summer place now, and Maine's coastline was her idea of Paradise. She looked at a number of houses and cottages, but none of them suited her. They were either too rundown, too expensive, or built on uninteresting locations. Then a friend came up with the perfect solution, suggesting that she buy some land and build her own place. Carson found a piece of property that overlooked the estuary of the Sheepscot River at a point at which the water was deep enough to allow whales to swim by. Carson was enthusiastic; the house would take a year to build, but to her it would be worth the wait.

In the meantime, she told herself, she would simply work on the shoreline book. Unfortunately, what had sounded simple in theory proved difficult in execution. The writing was agonizingly slow, and she started the project over several times, hoping that working from a new point of view would open the floodgates of her creative dam. She became frustrated and angry with her lack of progress, but she kept at it. She never gave up. She kept pecking at the typewriter, and in between she did a little traveling to Florida and South Carolina.

As if completing the book wasn't enough of a worry for her, she also went through a family crisis. Her niece, Marjorie, had a baby. None of the Carsons had much to say about the birth. Carson told friends that Marjorie had been briefly married and become pregnant before the divorce, but the truth is hidden in the shadows of time; no one knows who the father was or what became of him. Marjorie had inherited diabetes from her mother, which can sometimes make giving birth a risky event, but her son, Roger, was born with no complications.

When the summer of 1953 came, Carson packed up her mother and her cat and drove to her new seasonal home in Maine. She loved the place even more than she had thought she would. From the large picture windows that faced the mouth of the estuary, she could watch seals, otters, dolphins, and even the occasional whale among the waves. The sky was huge and glorious and full of seabirds. The quiet was calming and

Dorothy Freeman, a close friend and neighbor of Carson's in Maine, shared her love of nature. They worried about the overdevelopment of the local land and strove to save a beloved tract of forest next to Carson's property, which they called "the Lost Woods." Carson had some political clout as well, being the newly appointed chairperson of the Maine chapter of the Nature Conservancy.

nurturing. And best of all, perhaps, she made a friend—a woman named Dorothy Freeman.

Dorothy and Stan Freeman owned a place on nearby Southport Island. Dorothy was a nature lover, like Carson, with an open and warm heart. She and Carson bonded immediately. Unfortunately, the two didn't get to spend much time together in that year. Carson's mother was deteriorating with age and ill health and required constant looking after. Carson had little time to visit with anyone else. Still, she and Freeman kept close ties by writing to each other every day, and it wasn't long before they were expressing love for each other, like close sisters.

In the fall, Carson returned to her home in Maryland, but she kept up her correspondence with Freeman. She also spent time becoming more politically active. The Republicans had taken over the White House in January and were now making decisions about the use of public lands that were very favorable to people in big business. First, they had fired Albert M. Day, along with many other experienced people, from the Fish and Wildlife Service. Day had been a great conservationist in his tenure as head of the Service. Now he and the others would be replaced by political appointees. After that, the government decided to consider a proposal to create a dam that would flood some of the great Monument Parks in Colorado and Utah. Carson was outraged; she wrote letters and articles and did interviews, using her celebrity as a political tool to strengthen the position of the conservationists.

Through all the political turmoil and notoriety, she continued to struggle with the book. By June, she finally had finished a rough draft of *The Edge of the Sea* and sent a section of the book to *The New Yorker*. The magazine offered to buy serial rights, as it had done with *The Sea Around Us,* and ended up publishing the excerpt in two installments in August of 1956. The book itself finally made it into bookstores in October. Although it never reached #1 on the bestseller lists, it remained in the top 10 for over five months, finally reaching the #2 position.

AFTER *THE EDGE OF THE SEA*
Carson's day-to-day life seemed to settle down after the publication. The reviews were extremely satisfying, sales were strong, and she had many other projects in mind, including a small book on evolution for a series that would be published by

Harper & Brothers. However, two projects really grabbed her attention. The editors at *Women's Home Companion* had sent her a proposal to do a book for children, and the producers of *Omnibus*, a popular television series of the time, asked her to write a script for a program about clouds. She chose to work on the script first. Clouds, after all, were part of the same grand ecology that included the sea. The world was one place, and no scientist could pretend to separate one part of it from another.

The script was broadcasted under the title "Something About the Sky." Carson loved the result so much that she went out and bought herself a television. She had watched the broadcast at her brother's home; their relationship had gradually improved over the years, so that now they kept in steady contact.

After her television triumph, Carson tackled the children's article. She had great fun writing it because she had enlisted the help of her young grandnephew, Roger Christie, in deciding what to include and what to leave out. She had grown to deeply love Roger, almost as if she were his mother. It was only natural. After all, she cared for him most of the time. Marjorie's health problems had grown worse over the years, and Carson had assumed responsibility for caring for her and her son, especially during time of crisis.

When the article, "Help Your Child to Wonder," appeared in the pages of the *Companion*, nearly everyone Carson knew was moved to tears by it. Marie Rodell was so impressed with it—it was so personal, and loving, and itself full of wonder—that she suggested Carson expand it into a book. It was a good idea, Carson knew, but she had other projects to attend to first. She was still trying to figure out how she would approach the evolution book.

She had other distractions as well, and although she didn't realize it then, they would keep her from her writing for a very long time.

The summer of 1956 didn't start out badly. Carson went to her home in Maine, as usual. Her grandnephew, Roger, and his mother, Marjorie, came to visit as they had every year. But Carson's mother had ever-worsening health problems. Carson had planned to mix a little rest with a little work, as she always did, but her mother suffered a severe bout of arthritis, which demanded Carson's constant attention. It was difficult for Carson to find herself so much a servant to her mother's needs, but she did her best not to reveal the stress it put her under.

Her constant source of replenishment was her ever-closer friendship with Dorothy Freeman; she'd dedicated *The Edge of*

THE THALIDOMIDE SCANDAL

By the time *Silent Spring* was published, in 1962, many had already become deeply concerned that scientists were exposing humans to chemicals without really understanding the dangers involved. The most tragic example, the use of the drug thalidomide, inflamed public anger and boosted the sales of Carson's book.

Thalidomide, first sold in Germany, was prescribed both as a sedative and as a palliative for morning sickness in pregnant women, and it soon became popular throughout the world. Unfortunately, thalidomide had not been tested well for safety, so scientists hadn't realized that it could cause birth defects. Babies were born with flipper-like appendages in place of arms—the first in late 1956—and many also suffered brain damage. By the end of the crisis, 12,000 of these "thalidomide babies" had been born, and scientists estimate that another 8,000 had aborted spontaneously.

Most of these babies were born overseas, for the reviewing U.S. medical officer, Frances Kelsey, had refused to allow the drug into the country because she was suspicious of the testing standards. But the thalidomide scandal made American readers especially receptive to *Silent Spring*.

the Sea to Dorothy and Stan. She and Dorothy stole a few minutes to spend together whenever they could, but on their long walks together through the nearby countryside, Carson realized that another problem was creeping into her life: overdevelopment of the local land. She talked it over with Dorothy. There was one tract of forest adjacent to Carson's property that they particularly loved. They called it "the Lost Woods." They decided to make it their cause to save the area in its pristine condition. To do that, Carson would have to buy the land, which meant she would have to find a way to come up with a large sum of money. In the meantime, she would use whatever clout she had attained when she had accepted an appointment as chairperson of the Maine chapter of the Nature Conservancy a few weeks earlier.

THE DISTRACTIONS BEGIN

In October, the situation with her mother grew worse when Maria suffered a bad fall. It became immediately obvious that she wouldn't be able to get around on her own. This meant that Carson would have to be by her side nearly every second. Friends strongly recommended that a full-time nurse be hired, but Carson decided a housekeeper would be more of a help and hired one.

The situation deteriorated. Maria needed ever more attention, suffering with respiratory ailments, arthritis, and the pain from her fall. And now Marjorie, Carson's niece, was having more health problems associated with her diabetes. Carson did her best to help out and to look after Roger.

Then she had a brainstorm. She had two projects currently in the making: an *Anthology of Nature* for Simon & Schuster and a children's version of *The Sea Around Us*. She decided she would set up trust funds from the proceeds of both. One fund would be dedicated to saving the Lost Woods, the other to financially supporting Marjorie and Roger. That would effectively take care of two of the three problems she had been

Carson in this period became more of a caregiver than an author. Her mother's health problems, followed by her niece's diabetes and the needs of little Roger, kept her busy almost constantly and stood in the way of the work she wanted to accomplish. Domestic issues would occupy the year following Marjorie's death in 1957. This photograph dates to around 1922.

wrestling with in her personal life over the past few months.

Unfortunately, events quickly took away any sense of control that Carson thought she had developed. In mid-January, Marjorie came down with pneumonia, on top of an anemia that seemed unresponsive to drug treatment. She was rushed to the hospital and stabilized. Carson watched over Roger, who was also sick with a respiratory infection. In fact, Carson herself had begun to feel ill. Then everyone seemed to recover, even Marjorie to some extent, but she was not cured—she had been given only a reprieve. Within two weeks of her returning home from the hospital, she became ill again and declined quickly. On January 30, 1957, at the age of 31, Marjorie Christie died.

More Determined Than Ever: 1957–1960

[I]t seems reasonable to believe—and I do believe—that the more clearly we can focus our attention on the wonders and realities of the universe about us the less taste we shall have for the destruction of our race. Wonder and humility are wholesome emotions, and they do not exist side by side with a lust for destruction.
—Rachel Carson, accepting the
National Book Award for Nonfiction, 1963

THE DISTRACTIONS CONTINUE

Marjorie's death left the care of little Roger, now almost five years old, completely in Carson's hands. Neither Carson's brother, Robert, nor Marjorie's sister, Virginia, was willing to take on the responsibility. They had their own families to look after, and Robert had a mean streak in him where Roger was concerned. With Roger in the house, Carson felt the time had

After an extended period away from her writing, Carson (shown here in a file photo) was energized once again by a letter from an old journalist friend, Olga Owens Huckins of Duxbury, Massachusetts. Huckins's moving description of the fatal effects of pesticides stirred Carson to take up the struggle once more, and she began her activist work in earnest.

come to find a more spacious place to live. All these years she had rented her home, but she could find no rentals that pleased her around Silver Spring, so she bought a lot nearby, hired a construction company, and commenced building.

She spent the next year dealing exclusively with the house

construction, her mother, and Roger, who proved to be such a trial that she thought about taking him to a psychiatrist. He shadowed her everywhere she went, and when she tried to work, he constantly interrupted her to get her attention. He had no friends his own age, and he was physically inept. She had enrolled him in a private school for a while, but she had to keep him home constantly because of illness—probably psychological in nature, according Carson's doctor, and due to his mother's death. The little boy she had always so loved was making a hell of her life, and she couldn't figure out what to do about it.

The only writing she managed to complete was an assignment to contribute an article to the magazine *Holiday* in 1958 on the nation's beaches. Her dream of saving the Lost Woods was evaporating before her eyes. She had contacted the owners about buying the place, but their price was far too steep for her.

TAKING ON "BIOCIDES"

To make matters worse, she was struggling with a sense of dread concerning the very topic that had been her passion all her life: the conservation of nature. Science had developed atomic bombs in the 1940s, and then moved on to discover the hydrogen bomb, a weapon of even greater destructive power. And now there had been this news about massive DDT spraying to kill fire ants.

Carson had done no serious writing for nearly two years when she received the letter from Olga Owens Huckins relating how destructive pesticide spraying had been in Massachusetts. Carson blamed her lack of productivity on her personal situation. All of her days had been filled with the distractions of her family. But perhaps, as had happened in an earlier period of her life, she had just been waiting for something to write about.

Huckins's letter set her on fire, and DeWitt Wallace's lack of interest in publishing anything about the problem fanned the flames—but his wasn't the only magazine that declined. Marie Rodell couldn't find *any* potential buyers. Everyone, it seemed, was afraid of losing income should advertisers from the chemical industry become disgruntled.

One editor, however, decided to take up the banner. This was William Shawn, and his magazine was the same that had had the foresight to purchase serial rights to all of Carson's previous work: *The New Yorker.*

In addition to an article, she had begun making plans to write a book. On the advice of Marie Rodell and Paul Brooks, Carson agreed to work with a collaborator on the idea, but the candidate, Edwin Diamond, a young, aggressive writer at the magazine *Newsweek,* proved unsatisfactory. She then changed her mind and decided go it alone. She ended her partnership with Diamond after four months, leaving him angry and embittered. In his place, she hired a research assistant, an old friend's daughter, named Bette Haney, who was attending Bryn Mawr College, a women's college outside of Philadelphia, and currently looking for a summer job.

Early in her research, Carson met Bob Rudd, a wildlife biologist who had gathered material on the ecological damage he had seen chemicals create over the previous five years. They instantly became fast friends, sharing information freely with each other. She also received information from Edward O. Wilson, an entomologist at Harvard University. He told her about field studies on spraying fire ants done by John George, a scientist, for the Fish and Wildlife Service two years earlier. George himself later became a prime source of material for her, as did many other scientists in the field, from bird experts to soil scientists.

A DOUBLE LOSS; CARSON'S HEALTH BEGINS TO FAIL

In the midst of all this activity, Carson lost the one friend who had been with her nearly every day of her life: her mother. On November 22, 1958, Maria Carson suffered a stroke. Although she survived the event, in her weakened state she contracted pneumonia. One week later, she died in the hospital, under an oxygen tent, with Carson holding her hand.

Maria had been a trial to her daughter over the past few years. She had needed constant attention; she had been jealous of anyone—excepting little Roger—to whom Carson had offered affection or friendship; and she had dominated every conversation within earshot—whether Carson was talking to a personal friend, a distinguished scientist, or an important writer. But through all this, Carson had loved her deeply and dearly. Her mother had always been there to support her and comfort her, to help ease Carson's life in any way she could, and to cheer her on to even greater accomplishment. If the discomforts of old age had made Maria difficult, she couldn't be blamed for that. Even now, she had taken up the banner against pesticides along with Carson, and not because she was an angry woman but because she so loved life in all its forms. To her daughter, Maria Carson had been a great woman.

Heartbroken at the loss, but more determined than ever, Carson continued her research on the environmental destructiveness of pesticides. Gradually, through various conservation organizations such as the National Wildlife Federation and the Audubon Society, the public was becoming aware of how dire a problem these poisons really created. In the meantime, the government began issuing propaganda in the form of public statements and "educational" films defending its massive use of toxins. They claimed that DDT was essentially a helpful chemical and did far more good than harm. Carson knew better. By now, her research had shown her that not only was it harmful to animals, but it could also cause nerve damage and cancer in humans.

In 1959, Carson wrote a brief letter of response to an editorial in *The Washington Post* that claimed declining bird populations were primarily due to a harsh winter the year before. Her letter demolished the editorialist's argument. She received many replies, but one especially pleased her. It was

Maria Carson, whose death foreshadowed her daughter's own failing health. She had been as fascinated by the natural world as Carson herself, and she'd provided Carson's early introduction to the life sciences. With age, though, Maria had become a financial, emotional, and physical burden; still, Carson had cared for her mother diligently, and they'd maintained a close bond. Losing her was a terrible blow.

from Agnes Meyer, the owner of *The Washington Post,* who indicated she was in total agreement with Carson. The two soon became close friends.

Carson hoped to get a fair amount of work done in Maine

that summer, but Roger came down with a lung ailment that obliged her to care for him constantly—and, once again at the mercy of someone else's illness, she accomplished little. When she returned to Maryland at the end of the season, she continued her research, which took her deeper and deeper into new scientific territory. By the end of the year, she had written seven chapters, including two on cancer, that she had come to believe would be the linchpin of her book. She felt strong and confident she would finish the book soon.

Once again, however, illness intervened, but this time it wasn't someone else's. Early in 1960, she was diagnosed with a duodenal ulcer—an inflammation and erosion in the lining of part of the small bowel. She changed her diet to bland foods and took antacids, and then got back to work. Her body still wouldn't cooperate. She immediately came down with a

THE EFFECTS OF DDT

From Olga Huckins's letter to Carson:

The 'harmless' shower bath killed seven of our lovely song-birds outright. We picked up the three dead bodies the next morning, right by the door. . . . The next day three were scattered around the bird bath. (I had emptied it and scrubbed it after the spraying, but YOU CAN NEVER KILL DDT.) On the following day one robin dropped suddenly from a branch in our woods.

We were too heart-sick to hunt for other corpses. All of these birds died horribly and in the same way: their bills gaping open and their splayed claws were drawn up to their breasts in agony. All summer long, every time we went into the garden, we were attacked by the most voracious mos-quitoes that had ever appeared there. But the grasshoppers, visiting bees, and other harmless insects, were all gone.

serious pneumonia and sinus infection. Carson struggled against her illnesses, slowly recovered, and once again returned to her project. But fate wasn't through with her yet. During her recovery from pneumonia, Carson had found some lumps in one breast, which meant she would have to have them removed and tested for cancerous tissue. Coincidentally, at the same time, she had submitted the two cancer chapters from the book to Paul Brooks, her editor, for review.

Although Carson entered the hospital simply to have cysts removed, she came out having gone through a radical mastectomy, the total removal of one breast, along with surrounding muscle tissue and lymph nodes. Her doctor had told her she had a condition that bordered on cancer, and he'd referred to the removal of her breast as simply a wise precaution.

In fact, he'd lied: Carson later learned that she had a cancerous tumor and that this tumor had already metastasized, or spread its cells to other parts of her body. Withholding bad news from patients was a common medical practice of the day, for doctors believed widely that truthful information could simply drive their patients to despair—but the truth would be undeniable within a year.

And No Birds Sing

Those who contemplate the beauty of the earth find reserves of
strength that will endure as long as life lasts.
—Rachel Carson, *The Sense of Wonder* (1965)

FULFILLING THE MISSION

Carson forced herself to return to her work. Over the next year,
she continued her slow but relentless efforts at the project,
along with other, shorter assignments, such as updating and
writing a new introduction to *The Sea Around Us*. In 1960, she
took a little time off to work in John F. Kennedy's campaign for
the presidency and serve on the Natural Resources Committee
of the Democratic Advisory Council.

In November, after her candidate's win, Carson discovered a
hard mass over her ribs, not far from the site of her mastectomy.
Because she had been deceived before about her condition by
doctors at George Washington University, she decided to take

her case to a cancer expert in Cleveland. This expert, Dr. George Crile, told her the brutal truth: that she had cancer and that her cancer had spread to her lymph nodes—a sign that she might not have long to live. He recommended that she undergo radiation treatment, as well as sterilization, in the hope of stopping her production of female hormones and thereby slowing the progress of disease.

The radiation treatments aggravated her ulcer and lowered her immunity, and she developed a serious staphylococcal infection in her bladder, which then spread to her joints, leaving her unable to walk for months. A serious eye inflammation followed.

Despite all these health setbacks, Carson went on doggedly with her research and writing. She spoke with a huge array of scientists, went through mountains of research material, sent her chapters out for review by experts and editors, wrote, rewrote, sent her chapter out again. It seemed as if the project would never reach its conclusion. But it did.

She finally finished her work in 1961. William Shawn at *The New Yorker* was so moved by the manuscript that he called her personally to tell her how good it was. Paul Brooks made a few editorial suggestions, but the work was done.

At the same time, she learned that her cancer had returned and had metastasized to, or spread through, much of her body. She was frightened at first, but then, inexplicably, she began to feel a kind of peace within herself. She had done what she had set out to do, fulfilled her mission: she had written her love of nature, and she had spoken out in defense of the natural world. Perhaps she had a limited amount of time left to live, but she was using her time well. What more could anyone ask from life but a life well lived? She consented to further radiation treatments—perhaps they would give her a little more time—but she was resigned to her fate.

THE AFTERMATH OF *SILENT SPRING*

When *The New Yorker* published *Silent Spring* in three installments, most readers responded as she'd wanted them to: outrage at the government's cavalier use of toxins in the environment. Carson was deluged with requests for personal appearances, but her health wouldn't allow it. Instead, she headed for Maine with Roger.

Even before the book was published in the following fall, the chemical industry and the U.S. Department of Agriculture went into an uproar of denial and counter-accusations, claiming that Carson's arguments were one-sided or misrepresented the chemical industry. Even government officials were leaking comments that they viewed Carson's book as unfair and unconvincing, and the government maintained its official position that insecticides were safe and effective.

The public was not fooled. The Department of Agriculture was buried under a torrent of letters complaining about dusting with DDT. However, Stewart Udall, the Secretary of the Interior under President Kennedy, was in full agreement with *Silent Spring*, and had been a supporter of Carson's work for many years. Partly because of his involvement, a high-level meeting of the chiefs of six government bureaus took place to discuss the use of pesticides and the government's involvement. A task force was appointed to investigate and report on the problem to the President.

Just before the book was to be published, a lawyer from one chemical company, Velsicol, wrote to Houghton Mifflin, stating that some of the book's claims disparaged Velsicol's products and were therefore actionable—grounds for a lawsuit. Both Carson and her publishers decided to ignore the threats, for they knew she stood on solid ground. Similar threats were made against *The New Yorker* and *Audubon*, with the same results.

Carson was now a more public figure than ever before. She did television and magazine interviews, and went through mountains of mail sent by concerned readers. She was characterized in articles as friend and foe, praised and condemned by the highest offices in the country. She even gave a seminar at the White House. She had become more famous than she had ever dreamed she would, but as she well knew, nature bows to no one. The cancer progressed. By December, she was again undergoing radiation treatments. Then, while shopping at a local department store in Maryland, she collapsed; it was obvious that her health was deteriorating. She did her best to keep her condition from the public. She would fight for every breath her life could give her.

Silent Spring was still on the bestseller lists, and the chemical industry was spending millions in trying to find ways to turn public opinion against the book. Carson found herself under attack by everything from baby food companies to garden clubs. Pamphlets were issued by pesticide companies, and scientists whom they funded railed in public forums against Carson. Her resolve never wavered.

CBS Reports, a television show hosted by Eric Sevareid, devoted a full hour to *Silent Spring* that year, exposing 15 million people to its message. The show proved so popular that CBS devoted another hour to *Silent Spring* a short time later. Again Carson's critics struck back like vipers, calling her a Communist and a spinster with no scientific credibility, but still she stood firm.

Finally, she was invited to testify before a Senate Committee chaired by Senator Abraham Ribicoff. She made her case against pesticides eloquently and convincingly. There was little doubt now that the government would take action. But it took a report by the President's Science Advisory Committee, recommending the orderly reduction of use of pesticides, to finally quiet the critics. Carson's case had been made and won.

Her strong belief in her position led her to make a trip to San Francisco, although she was barely healthy enough to survive it. She gave her speech, entitled "The Pollution of the Environment," from a wheelchair.

A LIFE WELL LIVED

Time was running out: despite all the treatments she tried, her cancer moved into her bones, and then affected her heart. She developed terrible chest pains that lasted for weeks, until

Carson testifying before a Senate subcommittee in June of 1963—
continuing, despite her failing health, to speak out against the
government's unadvised use of toxins. Her death would come
just two days later. But a report by the President's Science
Advisory Committee recommended a reduction in pesticide use—
Carson had won. Her name will forever be associated with the
environmental movement in the United States.

therapy finally helped to relieve her suffering. She seemed to be
developing new complications almost faster than she could
deal with them, but still she kept on.

She went to Maine that summer, but she needed the help
of a friend to look after Roger. In the fall, her doctors gently
told her that she had little time left. She spent some of it with
Marie Rodell, putting her papers in order so they might be
donated to a university. She spent a great deal of time trying
to find someone who could look after Roger after her death.
Eventually, that turned out to be Paul Brooks and his wife.
And she spent every moment she could find communicating
with her dear Dorothy Freeman, who had recently lost her
own husband to a heart attack.

Gradually, Carson succumbed. She was hospitalized for a

severe viral infection, and then came home, only to go through a long period of terrible, unremitting nausea. She then flew to the clinic in Cleveland for an operation that might slow the cancer's progress, but the operation did no good. Finally, she returned home to Silver Spring. There was nothing else to be done.

Freeman visited with her a few days later and remained as long as she could. Carson was drifting in and out of consciousness, but she was acutely aware of Freeman's presence. There was no one she would rather have been with. At the end of their visit, they each felt a kind of serenity and peace each other. No matter what happened now, they were prepared.

SILENT SPRING, THE ENVIRONMENT, AND THE LAW

Silent Spring was a wake-up call; before its publication, only one major law had ever been passed concerning the environment. This was a 1958 law, the Delaney Clause, that prohibited the addition of any element to processed food "if it is found to induce cancer when ingested by man or animal."

In the years after *Silent Spring*, though, came a flood of important environmental legislation: The Environmental Protection Agency (EPA) was established in 1969 to ensure that no governmental body acted upon the environment without first conducting a thorough study of the potential effects of its action. An agency was established soon thereafter to protect workers from toxins in the workplace, and in the next two years came acts setting standards for clean air and clean water. By 2002, regulations were in place for the handling of all known toxic materials. Especially in the wake of the terrorist attacks of September 11, public awareness of the dangers of chemicals became high—so no substance that posed a threat went unwatched for long.

Two days later, just before twilight on April 14, Carson's heart stopped beating. She was 56 years old.

In the years since her death, Rachel Carson's name has become synonymous with the environmental movement in the United States. She was the first really popular writer to bring environmental issues to the public's attention in a way that encouraged action, and the effect of her work has been enormous. Within years of the publication of *Silent Spring*, laws already were being passed to safeguard processed foods from carcinogens, to purify air and water, and to regulate the handling of toxic materials. No discussion of the origins of environmentalism is possible without reference to her work.

In 1980, she posthumously received the highest award the United States offers to civilians, the Presidential Medal of Freedom. The commemoration made to her on that day summarizes her achievement:

> Never silent herself in the face of destructive trends, Rachel Carson fed a spring of awareness across America and beyond. A biologist with a gentle, clear voice, she welcomed her audiences to her love of the sea, while with an equally clear voice she warned Americans of the dangers human beings themselves pose for their environment. Always concerned, always eloquent, she created a tide of environmental consciousness that has not ebbed.

Chronology

1907   Rachel Louise Carson is born on May 27 in Springdale, Pennsylvania to Robert Warden Carson and Maria McLean Carson.

1918   Publishes her first short story, "A Battle in the Clouds," in *St. Nicholas*, a children's magazine.

1924   Graduates from Parnassus High School in June; enters Pennsylvania College for Women in September.

1926   Changes major from English to zoology in her junior year.

1928   Graduates *magna cum laude* with a bachelor of science degree from Pennsylvania College for Women.

1928   Spends six weeks of the summer at the Marine Biological Laboratory in Woods Hole, Massachusetts.

1928   Begins her graduate work at Johns Hopkins University in Baltimore, Maryland.

1932   Graduates from Johns Hopkins with a master's degree in marine zoology.

1935   Assumes the financial responsibility of caring for her mother after her father dies of heart failure. Accepts a part-time job with the United States Bureau of Fisheries writing seven-minute radio scripts for a program called *Romance Under the Waters*.

1936   Passes the civil service exam to become a full-time junior aquatic biologist and becomes one of only two women working at the professional level at the Bureau of Fisheries. Publishes her first popular science article, "It'll Be Shad-Time Soon," in the Sunday magazine section of *The Baltimore Sun*. The article discusses the decline of the Chesapeake Bay shad fishery.

1937   Sister, Marian, dies of pneumonia. Rachel takes on the additional financial burden of caring for Marian's daughters, Marjorie and Virginia.

1937   Publishes "Undersea," an adaptation of some writing she had done for the Bureau of Fisheries, in *The Atlantic Monthly* in July. The article captures the attention of Quincy Howe, an editor at Simon & Schuster, who offers her a contract to write her first book.

1941   Publishes her first book, *Under the Sea-Wind,* with Simon & Schuster. It meets with critical success, but sales are disappointing.

1942   Promoted to assistant aquatic biologist in the newly created U.S. Fish and Wildlife Service.

1945   Publishes "The Bat Knew It First," a scientific comparison of modern radar with the bat's use of sonar to hunt, in *Collier's.*

1948   Promoted to full biologist and becomes editor-in-chief of the Information Division.

1951   Publishes *The Sea Around Us* with Oxford University Press, and the book becomes an instant bestseller.

1952   On the advice of her agent, Marie Rodell, Carson re-releases *Under the Sea-Wind,* which immediately joins *The Sea Around Us* on the bestseller list. Carson leaves the Fish and Wildlife Service to become a full-time writer.

1953   Carson and her mother move into the cottage Carson has recently had constructed on Southport Island, Maine.

1957   Niece, Marjorie Christie, dies, and Carson adopts Roger, Marjorie's five-year-old son.

1958   Mother dies. Receives letter from Olga Huckins describing a bird kill in her private sanctuary due to the spraying of DDT. Begins to research the effects of pesticides.

1960   Goes into the hospital for cyst removal, but has a radical mastectomy; is later told she has cancer.

1962   *Silent Spring* appears in serial form in *The New Yorker.* The chemical industry spends millions attacking Carson and the book.

1963   Cancer progresses; Carson continues treatment. CBS produces *The Silent Spring of Rachel Carson,* followed quickly by a sequel. Testifies before a Senate Committee hearing chaired by Senator Abraham Ribicoff.

1964   Dies on April 14 at her home in Silver Spring, Maryland. Her grandnephew, Roger Christie, is put under the care of Rachel's editor at Houghton Mifflin, Roger Brooks, and his wife.

Bibliography

Freeman, Martha, ed. *Always, Rachel: The Letters of Rachel Carson and Dorothy Freeman, 1952–1964: The Story of a Remarkable Friendship.* Beacon Press, 1999.

Lear, Linda. *Rachel Carson: Witness for Nature.* Henry Holt, 1997. The definitive biography.

Sterling, Philip. *Sea and Earth: The Life of Rachel Carson.* Thomas Y. Crowell Company, 1970.

Works by Rachel Carson

"Undersea," 1937

Under the Sea-Wind, 1941

The Sea Around Us, 1951

The Edge of the Sea, 1955

"Help Your Child to Wonder," 1956

"Our Ever-Changing Shore," 1957

Silent Spring, 1962

The Sense of Wonder, 1965

Further Reading

The American Experience: Rachel Carson's Silent Spring. PBS Video, 1992.

Brooks, Paul. *Rachel Carson: The Writer at Work.* Sierra Books, 1998. (Formerly published as *The House of Life,* 1972.) Brooks was Carson's editor and published this collection of Carson's writing; it remained the only source of information on Carson's life for many years.

Freeman, Martha: *Always, Rachel: The Letters of Rachel Carson and Dorothy Freeman, 1952–1964: The Story of a Remarkable Friendship.* Beacon Press, 1999.

Graham, Frank, Jr. *Since* Silent Spring. Houghton Mifflin, 1970.

Harlan, Judith. *Sounding the Alarm.* Dillon Press, 1989.

Hynes, Patricia H. *The Recurring Silent Spring.* Pergamon Press, 1989.

Lear, Linda. *Rachel Carson: Witness for Nature.* Henry Holt, 1997. The definitive biography.

———, ed. *Lost Woods: The Discovered Writing of Rachel Carson.* Beacon Press, 1998. Anthology of Carson's unpublished writings.

Lee, Sally. *Pesticides.* Franklin Watts, 1991.

Reef, Catherine. *Rachel Carson: The Wonder of Nature* (Earth Keepers Series). Henry Holt, 1992.

Stwertka, Eve. *Rachel Carson.* Franklin Watts, 1991.

Waddell, Craig, ed. *And No Birds Sing: Rhetorical Analyses of Rachel Carson's* Silent Spring. Southern Illinois University Press, 2000. A collection of new and revised essays examining Carson's language in *Silent Spring.*

Wadsworth, Ginger. *Rachel Carson: Voice for the Earth.* Lerner Publications, 1992.

Websites
The Rachel Carson Homestead
www.rachelcarsonhomestead.org

Linda Lear's RachelCarson.org
www.rachelcarson.org

Chatham College: The Rachel Carson Institute
www.chatham.edu/rci/

Rachel Carson National Wildlife Refuge
rachelcarson.fws.gov

State of Pennsylvania: The Rachel Carson Forum
www.dep.state.pa.us/dep/Rachel_Carson/Rachel_Carson.htm

Ecology Hall of Fame: Rachel Carson
www.ecotopia.org/ehof/carson/

The Rachel Carson Council
members.aol.com/rccouncil/ourpage/index.htm

The North Carolina National Estuarine Research Reserve
www.ncnerr.org

EnviroHealthAction
www.envirohealthaction.org

Pesticide Action Network International
www.pan-international.org

University of Nebraska: Pesticide Education Resources
pested.unl.edu

Northwest Coalition for Alternatives to Pesticides (NCAP)
www.pesticide.org/default.htm

Environmental Protection Agency: Office of Prevention,
    Pesticides, and Toxic Substances
www.epa.gov/oppts/

Environmental Protection Agency: Office of Pesticide Programs
www.epa.gov/pesticides/

Beyond Pesticides
www.beyondpesticides.org

Pesticide Action Network: Pesticide Database
www.pesticideinfo.org

"Flying Dreams": A Tribute to St. Nicholas
www.mindspring.com/~jlyoung/nick.htm

Index

Index

and love of nature, 23-26, 32
and mentors, 36-38, 39, 40-41,
  43-44, 53, 55
and move to Chicago, 66-67
and move to Tacoma Park,
  Maryland, 67
and move to Woods Hole,
  Massachusetts, 82
and moving family to Silver
  Spring, Maryland, 58-59
and moving family to Steamer's
  Run (Baltimore), 45, 46, 47, 48
and political involvement, 85, 88,
  98
and poor health, 67, 73, 89, 96-97,
  98-100, 101-105
and prospects for job outside
  government, 66-69
and start of research on pesticides,
  12-21, 92-93
and summer internships, 41-43,
  48
as teacher, 48, 55, 63
and travels for government, 70-71,
  72-73
and TV script, 86
and vacation in cottage in
  Maine, 71-72
and vacation near U.S. Fisheries
  Station (North Carolina),
  60-62
and work for government, 52-58,
  53, 56, 61, 63, 66-68, 70-71,
  72-73, 76, 82
and zoology master's degree, 40,
  41, 43, 44-48
Carson, Robert (brother), 28, 45,
  47, 48, 52, 86
Carson, Robert (father)
  burial of, 50-52
  death of, 49
  and move to Maryland, 45, 48

and poor health, 43
and poverty of family, 25, 26-27,
  31-32, 33-34
Carson's Grove, 22-23
CBS Reports, 102
Chincoteague, Virginia, Carson's
  trip to, 70
Christie, Marjorie (niece), 58, 66,
  83, 88, 89
Christie, Roger (grandnephew), 83,
  86, 88, 89, 94, 96, 101, 103
Collier's, 68
Conrad, Joseph, 35
Conservation Foundation, 18
Conservation in Action, 70-71,
  72-73
Coolidge, Cora, 34-35, 40, 43
Cowles, Reinhart P., 43, 44
Croft, Grace, 39

Day, Albert M., 70, 85
DDT, 13, 14-15
  Reader's Digest rejecting Carson's
    article on, 13, 56, 69, 92
  See also Pesticides
Diamond, Edwin, 93
Distinguished Service Medal, 80
Dodge, Mary Mapes, 28
Dutch elm disease, DDT used
  against, 14-15

Edge of the Sea, The, 81-82, 83, 85,
  87-88
Englicode, The, 39
Europe, DDT used in, 14

"Famous Sea Fight, A," 30
Fire ants, pesticides used against,
  12, 16, 92
Freeman, Dorothy, 15-16, 84-85,
  87-88, 103, 104
Frye, Mary, 42-43

Index

Index

Picture Credits

Contributors

E.A. TREMBLAY has been in publishing for 25 years. He has written two novels and six plays and ghostwritten three books, and he has taught writing for 10 years. He has also served as Senior Editor at two publishing houses and edited over a hundred books of fiction, science, history, philosophy, health, self-improvement, and communication. He studied International Relations at St. Joseph's University in Philadelphia.

JILL SIDEMAN, PH.D. serves as vice president of CH2M HILL, an international environmental-consulting firm based in San Francisco. She was among the few women to study physical chemistry and quantum mechanics in the late 1960s and conducted over seven years of post-doctoral research in high-energy physics and molecular biology. In 1974, she co-founded a woman-owned environmental-consulting firm that became a major force in environmental-impact analysis, wetlands and coastal zone management, and energy conservation. She went on to become Director of Environmental Planning and Senior Client Service Manager at CH2M HILL. An active advocate of women in the sciences, she was elected in 2001 as president of the Association for Women in Science, a national organization "dedicated to achieving equity and full participation for women in science, mathematics, engineering and technology."